Concepts in Bioinformatics
From Basics to Advanced

NIPA® GENX ELECTRONIC RESOURCES & SOLUTIONS P. LTD.
New Delhi-110 034

About the Editors

Dr. Chandra Sekhar Mukhopadhyay, CS Mukhopadhyay is a Senior Scientist at the College of Animal Biotechnology, Guru Angad Dev Veterinary and Animal Sciences University, Ludhiana. He has 15 years of working experience in research and teaching UG, PG, and Ph.D. students in bioinformatics, Genomics, and Animal Genetics. Dr. Mukhopadhyay has been engaged in research works involving animal genomics and transcriptomics directed toward the reproduction and disease resistance of cattle, buffalo, and chicken. He has earned three extra-murally funded research projects to his credit. He has undergone 6 months advanced training program on Marker Assisted Selection and Genomics at the Iowa State University (ISU), Ames, USA, during 2011-12. He is a Fulbright fellow (FNAPE) and has worked at ISU, in the area of Biostatistical modeling of imprinted loci in bovines. He has authored a book on bioinformatics published by John Wiley and Sons, USA. He is one of the national-level trainers on genome-wide association studies and genomic selection in training programs in India. Dr. Mukhopadhyay and his team have worked on bubaline micro-RNAs associated with diseases. He is currently working on parentage determination in bovines and canines.

Dr. Nisha Singh is Assistant Professor (Bioinformatics) at Gujarat Biotechnology University, Gandhinagar. Dr. Singh holds MSc. in Bioinformatics (OUAT, Bhubaneswar), a Ph.D. Biotechnology and Bioinformatics (NIPB, New Delhi) (2018). Dr. Singh obtained her post-doctoral training from the Institute of Genomic Diversity, Cornell University, Ithaca, New York, USA (2018-2020). Dr. Singh served as DST-Inspire Faculty at National Institute for Plant Biotechnology, New Delhi (2020-2022). Her research interests lie in Genomics, Proteomics, and Bioinformatics. She is especially interested in developing cost-effective, high-throughput genotyping technologies for genetics and molecular breeding applications in diverse species. Dr. Singh developed the first patented genic 50K SNP genotyping chip "OsSNPnks", a single copy gene-based SNP genotyping chip for genetics and molecular breeding applications in rice. Dr. Singh worked on several international genome sequencing projects including Wild rice, Wheat, Mango, Jute, Pigeonpea, and Tea. During her research career, she got several scholarships and awards. She has published more than 60 International research publications in reputed journals, h-index = 19, and 3 patents and 2 books. She is an active member of many international scientific societies and organizations, a Member of the American Society of Plant Biology, USA, Fellow of the Linnean Society of London. Dr. Singh has served as a reviewer and editor for several prestigious international journals including Nature, Springer, Elsevier,

BMC Genomics, Bioinformatics, Frontier in Plant Science, MDPI (Genes, Plants, agronomy) Journal of Food Science & Technology, omics group, and PLOSOne. For her scientific contribution, she gained several prestigious awards and honors (>20) such as the INSA-Medal for Young Scientist Award-2020 from the Indian National Science Academy, New Delhi, India, National Environmental Science Academy -2022, Scientist of the Year Award, and NASI- Young Scientist Platinum Jubilee Award 2022, Allahabad, India.

Prof (Dr) Yashpal Singh Malik is the Dean of the College of Animal Biotechnology, Guru Angad Dev Veterinary and Animal Sciences University, Ludhiana, India. Previously he served as "ICAR National Fellow" at the ICAR-Indian Veterinary Research Institute. His areas of expertise are virus characterization, viral disease epidemiology, microbial biodiversity, host-virus interactions, and pathogen diagnostics. He has pursued advanced studies in molecular virology at the University of Minnesota, USA; the University of Ottawa, Ontario, Canada; and the Wuhan Institute of Virology, Wuhan, China. He is the recipient of several prestigious awards and honors, including the ICAR-Jawaharlal Nehru Award. He has been awarded the prestigious Fellowship by the Academy of Microbiological Sciences, National Academy of Dairy Sciences, National Academy of Veterinary Science, and National Academy of Biological Sciences. Prof Malik has served as a member of the International Committee on Taxonomy of Viruses (ICTV) on the Birnaviridae and Picobirnaviridae. He has been associated with societies of international repute, like, the World Society for Virology (USA); the World Veterinary Association (WVA), and the Federation of Asian Veterinary Association (FAVA). He has been serving as Secretary General of the Indian Virological Society. He has authored 9 books, 60 book chapters, and over 200 research and review articles.

Concepts in Bioinformatics
From Basics to Advanced

Chandra Sekhar Mukhopadhyay
Senior Scientist
College of Animal Biotechnology
Guru Angad Dev Veterinary and Animal Sciences University
Ludhiana, Punjab

Nisha Singh
Assistant Professor (Bioinformatics)
Gujarat Biotechnology University
Gandhinagar, Gujarat

Yashpal Singh Malik
Dean
College of Animal Biotechnology
Guru Angad Dev Veterinary and Animal Sciences University
Ludhiana, Punjab

NIPA® GENX ELECTRONIC RESOURCES & SOLUTIONS P. LTD.
New Delhi-110 034

Mukhopadhyay C.S., Singh N. and Malik Y.S. 2024. Concepts in Bioinformatics: From Basics to Advanced. Pages, 84. NIPA® Genx Electronic Resources & Solutions P. Ltd., New Delhi-110034

NIPA® GENX ELECTRONIC RESOURCES & SOLUTIONS P. LTD.
101,103, Vikas Surya Plaza, CU Block
L.S.C.Market, Pitam Pura, New Delhi-110 034
Ph : +91 11 27341616, 27341717, 27341718
E-mail: newindiapublishingagency@gmail.com
www: www.nipabooks.com

For customer assistance, please contact
Phone: + 91-11-27 34 17 17
Fax: + 91-11- 27 34 16 16
E-Mail: feedbacks@nipabooks.com

ISBN: 978-93-95763-81-3

Composed and Designed by NIPA®.

Dedication to
The book is humbly dedicated to
the students, researchers, and professionals
in the field of biotechnology

Acknowledgments

The authors thankfully acknowledge all the persons who have contributed to the book in one or another form. Our sincere gratitude is expressed to the staff of the publishers who deserve a special note of thanks. Besides, our sincere thanks to the reviewer of the chapters and their critical comments to give a proper edge to the readers of the book. The authorities of Guru Angad Dev Veterinary and Animal Sciences University deserve special mention for providing a conducive environment for its faculty to excel in the global arena through research, academic, and extension activities.

Preface

Bioinformatics is an extremely important field of biological science that also includes in-depth knowledge and skill in statistics and computer science. With the advance of new sequencing projects, bioinformatics helps to comprehend biological processes to primarily serve the agriculture and healthcare sectors with various spinoffs. To address the advances and awareness in bioinformatics to students and researchers this book will serve as a quick reference book on the subject. Bioinformatics is essential in all the fields of biotechnology and molecular biology that deal with molecular data. Thus the subject caters to divergent disciplines of biological science. The book on Concepts in Bioinformatics, Basics to Advances is a compilation of basic information on bioinformatics and also includes advanced areas that are required by students and professionals. The authors have great knowledge and experience in putting together updated information on animal biotechnology through eminent experts.

The beginning of the book familiarizes the readers with the concept of bioinformatics and its history. Then some important concepts of basic bioinformatics have been discussed in the subsequent five chapters, that includes, databases, multiple sequence alignment, primer designing, and molecular phylogeny. This section is important to the postgraduate students of bioinformatics, biotechnology, and molecular biology. Chapters 9 to chapter 14 discusses BLAST and FASTA, protein structure prediction through homology modeling and molecular modeling, which are equally important for acquiring skills for in silico analysis. The last three chapters of the book discuss some advanced components of bioinformatics, namely, drug designing, systems biology, and synthetic biology. In general, the book is meant as a "short introduction" to bioinformatics and can be used as a sensitizer to study the subject.

The book provides a comprehensive introduction to the field of bioinformatics, covering a range of topics from basic concepts to advanced techniques. The book is aimed at students, researchers, and educators in the field of biotechnology and bioinformatics, and is designed to be a valuable resource for those just starting out in the field. The topics covered in the book include molecular data analysis, multiple sequence alignment, primer design, phylogenomics, omics, molecular modeling, drug design, and synthetic biology. Overall, it seems like the book would be a useful tool for anyone looking to gain a solid foundation in the field of bioinformatics.

Editors

Contents

Acknowledgments .... *ix*
Preface .... *xi*
List of Abbreviations .... *xv*

1. What is Bioinformatics 1
2. History of Bioinformatics 5
3. History of Programming Languages 9
4. Databases 15
5. Sequence Alignment 19
6. Molecular Phylogeny 25
7. Primer Designing 29
8. Primer Designing for qPCR (SYBR Green Chemistry) 33
9. Basic Local Alignment Search Tool (BLAST) 35
10. Fasta 39
11. Omics 41
12. Protein Structure 47
13. Homology Modeling 51
14. Molecular Modeling 55
15. Drug Designing 57
16. Systems Biology 63
17. Synthetic Biology 67

List of Abbreviations

AI	Artificial Intelligence
ALGOL	Algorithmic Language
ARPANET	Advanced Research Projects Agency Network
BBN	Bayesian Belief Network
BCPL	Basic Combined Programming Language
BISTI	Biomedical Information Science and Technology Initiative
BLAST	Basic Local Alignment Search Tool
BLOSUM	Blocks Amino Acid Substitution Matrix
CAP	Cap Analysis Gene Expression
CATH	Class, Architecture, Topology, and Homologous Super-family
CNVs	Copy Number Variations
COBOL	Common Business-Oriented Language
DDBJ	DNA Data Bank of Japan
DIP	Database of Interacting Proteins
DL	Deep Learning
ENA	European Nucleotide Archive
FORTRAN	Formula Translation
GEO	Gene Expression Omnibus
ME	Minimum Evolution
ML	Machine Learning
ML	Maximum Likelihood
NCBI	National Center For Biotechnology Information
NIH	National Institute of Health
NLS	Online System
OTU	Operational Taxonomic Unit
PAM	Point Accepted Mutation Matrices
PDB	Protein Data Bank
PHI-BLAST	Position Hit Initiated Blast

1

What is Bioinformatics

Abstract

Bioinformatics is an important interdisciplinary field that brings together several areas of science, including molecular biology, biostatistics, and computer science (vis-à-vis information technology). With the rapid increase in the sequencing of DNA/RNA/protein molecules, as well as the growing understanding of the interconnections between different areas of biological science, the importance of bioinformatics is only increasing. This chapter seems to provide a thorough introduction to the definition, concept, and importance of bioinformatics. It also appears to highlight the relevance and potential scope of the subject for students interested in pursuing a career in the field. As bioinformatics continues to evolve and expand, it is likely to become an increasingly important area of research and development in the life sciences.

Introduction

It is a branch of science that interprets biological data with the help of statistics, computer science, mathematics, and engineering. Bioinformatics makes use of computer systems and information technology, programming languages/tools, and applications vis-à-vis statistical knowledge for analyzing molecular data to explore systems biology and other information in biological sciences. Frank Tekaia defined bioinformatics as "The mathematical, statistical, and computing methods that aim to solve biological problems using DNA and amino acid sequences and related information". One popular definition of bioinformatics has been given by NIH BISTI Consortium: "Research development or application of computational tools and approaches for expanding the use of biological, medical, behavioral or health data including those to acquire, store, organize, archive, analyze or visualize such data". While Oxford dictionary defines bioinformatics as "Conceptualizing biology, in terms of molecules (in sense of physical chemistry) and applying informatics techniques (derived from disciplines viz. maths, computer science, and statistics) to understand and organize the information associated with these molecules, on a large scale".

Year-wise inclusion of various databases and users in NCBI

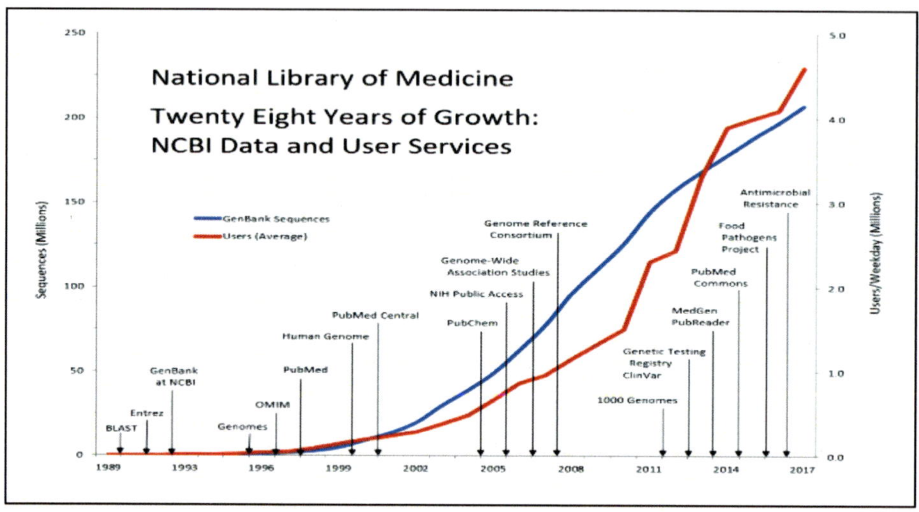

Sources: https://www.nlm.nih.gov/about/2019CJ.html

Why to study bioinformatics?

Bioinformatics is an upcoming science that has huge prospects. In this era of next-generation sequencing and advanced molecular biology, knowledge of bioinformatics is a must to analyze molecular data and interpret the results. Knowledge of advanced computer programming (using Hadoop, Scala, Spark, SQL, etc; the list is reasonably big) is needed to handle big data and databases. The following graph indicates how the volume of molecular databases has increased exponentially over time.

This is the time of artificial intelligence and machine learning. So, knowledge of bioinformatics, and computer programming is inevitable to make use of the biological data for unearthing the hidden treasure of information using AI-ML-DL.

What are the required skills to excel in bioinformatics?

Bioinformatics is the portmanteau of Biology + Informatics. Where **biology** is the science of life and living organisms, including their structure, function, growth, origin, evolution, and distribution. **Informatics** is the science of information that comprises **information processing** and the **engineering of information systems**. Informatics studies the **structure, algorithms, behavior**, and **interactions** of natural and artificial systems that **store, process, access, and communicate information**.

So, a student of bioinformatics needs to garner him/herself in biological sciences, computer sciences, and biostatistics. The thorough knowledge of biology makes a bioinformatician different from a computer programmer/computer engineer, while the knowledge of biostatistics and computer sciences gives a unique blend that a true biology professional lacks.

Who can study bioinformatics?

Any student who has passed 10+2 in higher grades (considering the competition in marks) can study B.Sc or B.Tech. Bioinformatics (3/4 years). Please go through https://www.biotecnika.org/2019/04/bioinformatics-career-scope/ to update yourself on the scope of bioinformatics in terms of job and research perspectives.

Are bioinformatics, computational biology, biostatistics, and biometrics same? If not, how these are different from each other?

Biostatistics is the scientific methodology of **collection, compilation,** and **interpretation of numerical facts** relating to biological sciences. Biometrics refers to the **collection, synthesis, analysis,** and **management of data** in biology. On the other hand, the terms bioinformatics and computational biology are used alternatively and refer to the application of computer programming and relevant biostatistical knowledge to analyze molecular data to unveil valuable information it. Bioinformatics is not limited to molecular data analysis, but also to storing, archiving, editing, or sharing data and information through online databases.

2

History of Bioinformatics

Abstract

This chapter provides a brief overview of the key milestones in the development of bioinformatics that would help to understand the historical context and evolution of a subject. As an interdisciplinary field, bioinformatics has grown gradually from molecular biology, with the development of various algorithms, databases, and other important tools that have helped to advance computational biology. Some important events in the history of bioinformatics might include the development of the first algorithms for sequence alignment and comparison, the creation of early databases such as GenBank and Swiss-Prot, and the development of software tools for molecular modeling and drug design. Other key milestones might include the sequencing of the first genomes, the development of high-throughput sequencing technologies, and the emergence of new areas of research such as systems biology and synthetic biology. By understanding the historical context of bioinformatics, students and researchers can gain a deeper appreciation for the current state of the field and the ongoing efforts to advance our understanding of the molecular mechanisms that underlie life.

Important

- 1933- Electrophoresis technique was introduced by Tiselius for separating proteins in solution
- 1936- Turing machine, an abstract machine developed by Alan Turing, with others developed the modern notion of algorithm
- 1940 - Austbury published the first X-Ray crystallography of DNA
- 1942 - A Fast Fourier Transform algorithm developed by G.C. Danielson and Cornelius Lanczos
- 1951- Pauling and Corey proposed the structure for the alpha-helix and beta-sheet (*PNAS*, **27**: 205-211, 1951; *PNAS*, **37**: 729-740, 1951)
- 1953- Watson and Crick reported the double helix model of DNA (Nat., 1953, 171: 737-738)

- 1955- Bovine insulin, the first protein sequenced and analyzed by F. Sanger
- 1958- American electrical engineer Jack St. Clair Kilby constructed the first integrated circuit at Texas Instruments. His work was recognized for the award of Nobel Prize in Physics in 2010.
- 1960- Doug Engelbart prototypes an "oNLine System" (NLS) which could do hypertext browsing editing, email, and invented the mouse
- 1969- The ARPANET (Advanced Research Projects Agency Network) was established by linking computers at the University of California, Los Angeles, Stanford, UCSB, and The University of Utah.
- 1970- Publication of Needleman-Wunsch algorithm for sequence alignment
- 1971- Invention of email program by Raymond Samuel Tomlinson at the Bolt, Beranek, and Newman (i.e. BBN Technologies)
- 1972- Creation of the first rDNA molecule (recombinant DNA) by Paul Berg and team
- 1975- Foundation of the "Microsoft Corporation" by Bill Gates and Paul Allen in New Mexico
- 1977- First DNA sequence analysis software was developed by Staden, followed by SeqAid in 1984
- 1978- Margaret O Dayhoff introduced point-accepted mutation matrices (i.e. PAM matrices)
- 1978- Tom Truscott, Jim Ellis, and Steve Bellovin established the first UseNet connection between Duke University in Durham and the University of North Carolina
- 1980- Complete gene sequence of FX-174 (5386 bases) was published.
- 1982- NCBI GenBank released three medical papers
- 1984- Margaret O Dayhoff developed the first online database "Protein Information resource"
- 1987- Applications of yeast artificial chromosomes (YAC) were described by David T. Burke and team (*Science*, **236**: 806-812).
- 1987- Publication of the physical map of *Escherichia coli* by Y. Kohara and team (*Cell* **51:** 319-337).

- 1987- Practical extraction report language (Perl) was released by Larry Wall as a Unix scripting language for text extraction.
- 1988- Establishment of the National Center for Biotechnology Information (NCBI) at the National Cancer Institute.
- 1988- Beginning of the Human Genome Initiative (Commission on Life Sciences, National Research Council. *Mapping and Sequencing the Human Genome*, National Academy Press: Washington, D.C.)
- 1988- Pearson and Lipman published the FASTA algorithm for sequence comparison
- 1990- Initial Worldwide Web program development continues on the NeXT (TBL)
- 1990- "what you see is what you get" (WYSIWYG) browser/editor with direct inline creation of links developed
- 1990- The first web server nxoc01.cern.ch was developed.
- 1990- The BLAST program (Altschul *et al.*1990) was designed
- 1991- Expressed sequence tags (ESTs) were described by J. Craig Venter and team (*Science*, **252**: 1651-1656).
- 1991- Myriad Genetics Institute (Utah) proposed to sequence human genes (BRCA1, BRACA1, CHD1, CtlP, p16, p19, MMAC1, MTS2, MMSC1, MMSC2)
- 1992- Craig Venter established the Institute for Genomic Research (TIGR)
- 1995- Microsoft released version 1.0 of Internet Explorer.
- 1994- EMBL established at Hinxton, UK
- 1996- Genome of *Saccharomyces cerevisiae* was sequenced (12.1 Mb)
- 1996- The Prosite database was created by Bairoch and his team
- 1996- The first commercial DNA chips produced by Affymetrix
- 1996- Structural Bioinformatics, Inc. was founded in San Diego, California.
- 2000- *D. melanogaster* genome sequence published
- 2001- First draft of human genome project published (Science, 2001, 1304-1351)

- 2003- The much coveted human genome project was completed
- 2004- Completion of the draft genome sequencing of the brown Norway laboratory rat (*Rattus norvegicus*) by the Rat Genome Sequencing Project Consortium.
- 2011- Google developed the popular open-source web programming language Dart

3

History of Programming Languages

Abstract

The knowledge of programming language(s) is necessary to solve biocomputational problems and also understand the data pattern. Computer programming is used to develop software to extract information from data which is very crucial while practicing bioinformatics. Programming language is a man-made, computer-understandable, artificial language, that is designed to instruct a machine, particularly a computer to get the desired output. This chapter briefly narrates the concept of algorithms, programming languages, and the historical perspective of the same.

Introduction

The term **algorithm** refers to a stepwise set of instructions, that are followed (by a machine or human) to do analysis or precise task, while **iterations** mean repeated execution of one task.

- **First Generation Programming Languages**: the machine-level languages, now not used. The data are entered through the front panel system of the computer system.
- **Second Generation Programming Languages**: These are assembly languages in which the codes are read and written by a programmer and assembled (by converting into a machine-readable form) to run on a computer: a process called assembly. The 2nd GPLs are used in kernels and device drivers, extremely intensive processing (viz. games, graphics, etc).
- **Third Generation Programming Languages**: These are programmer-friendly and more refined versions of the 2GPLs. 3GPLs are also called High-Level Languages. Better support towards aggregate data types is received through 3 GPL as these languages are easy to express concepts and ideas and interpret real-world problems. The codes are easier to read, write and maintain and are translated to machine-level languages by compiler and interpreter.
    - Examples: ALGOL, COBOL, FORTRAN, later, C, C++, C#, Java, etc.

- **Fourth Generation Programming Languages**: It's an improved version of the 3GLs that attempts to get closer to human language, the form of thinking, and conceptualization. 4GPLs are the class of non-procedural, high-level specification programming language or environment. 4GPLs attempt to help quickly develop programming that effectively generates highly complicated general-purpose 3GL instructions.

  Examples: SQL, R, SPSS, SAS, etc.

- **Fifth Generation Programming Languages**: The concept of 5GPL is entirely different from that of the 4GPL, as the 5GPL is used to solve problems through the constraints given to the program. The programmer need not develop the specific algorithm, as such, for a specific problem, rather s(he) is concerned with the type of problem assigned and the conditions imposed during problem-solving. Artificial intelligence is the main concern in developing 5GPLs.

  Example: Prolog, OPS5, and Mercury

History of Programming Languages

- 1801: Jacquard loom machine used holes in punched cards for sewing loom arm movements
- 1842-43: Ada Lovece devised a method to calculate the Bernoulli numbers using Analytical Engine invented by Charles Babbage: It is considered the first-ever programming language
- 1940s: the first modern computers were produced
- Assembly languages: the limited speed and memory capacity forced programmers to write assembly language programs
- 1943: Plankalkül, a programming language was designed (published in 1948, but not implemented) by Konrad Zuse
- 1943: ENIAC (Electric Numerical Integrator and Computer), the machine-specific code set was written. It appeared in 1948
- 1955: FORTRAN (FORmula TRANslator) was invented by John Backus et al.
- 1958: LISP (LISt Processor) was invented by John McCarthy et al.
- 1959: COBOL (COmmon Business Oriented Language) was created by the Short Range Committee, which was heavily influenced by Grace Hopper.

- 1963: CPL (forerunner to C): Combined Programming Language, a multi-paradigm programming language, designed by Christopher Strachey et al. It was influenced by ALGOL-60.
- 1964: PL/I (Programming Language One): a procedural, imperative computer programming language designed by IBM, for scientific, engineering, business, and systems programming applications
- 1967: BCPL (forerunner to C): Basic Combined Programming Language is a procedural, imperative, and structured computer programming language designed by Martin Richards
- 1969: B (forerunner to C): developed at Bell Labs. by Ken Thompson (along with Dennis Ritchie)
- 1970: Pascal:
    - is a small and efficient vis-à-vis a procedural programming language,
    - It was designed by Niklaus Wirth.
    - encourage good programming practices through data structuring and developing structured programming.
- 1972: C language:
    - is a general-purpose programming language
    - initially developed by Dennis Ritchie between 1969 and 1973 at AT&T Bell Labs.
    - Many later languages have borrowed directly or indirectly from C, including C#, D, Limbo, LPC, Java, JavaScript, Go, Perl, PHP, Python, and Unix's C shell
- 1978: SQL (initially only a query language, later extended with programming constructs):
    - SQL, a commercial programming language and is also one of the initial commercial programs, that has been used to manage data in relational DBMS.
    - SQL makes use of the relational model of Edgar F. Codd ("A Relational Model of Data for Large Shared Data Banks", 1970).
- 1980: C++ (as C with classes):
    - is a multi-paradigm, compiled, statically typed, and general-purpose programming language.

- C++ is an "intermediate-level language": a combination of both high-level and low-level language features
- Bjarne Stroustrup developed C++ (1979) at AT&T, Bell Labs.
- C++ was originally named as "C with Classes". Later it was renamed as "C++" (in 1983).

- 1983: Ada:
  - It is a statically typed, imperative, structured, and broad-spectral object-oriented high-level computer programming language.
  - Ada is extended from Pascal and other languages.
  - It has built-in language support for explicit concurrency, offering tasks, synchronous message passing, protected objects, and non-determinism.
  - Ada has been originally developed by Jean Ichbiah. The name "Ada" has been obtained after the name of the first computer programmer Ada Lovelace (1815–1852).
- 1984: MATLAB:
  - Developed by Jack Little and Steve Bangert after founding MathWorks in California in 1984.,
  - MATLAB is used for biostatistical analysis, matrix manipulations, and further advanced analyses.
- 1987: Perl:
  - is a high-level, interpreted, general-purpose, dynamic programming language.
  - Larry Wall developed Perl in 1987 as a general-purpose Unix scripting language for report processing and text parsing.
  - Different programming features are included in Perl from C, shell scripting (sh), AWK, and sed languages.
- 1991: Python:
  - It is a general-purpose, interpreted high-level programming language whose design philosophy emphasizes code readability.
  - Its syntax is said to be clear and expressive.
  - Python has a large and comprehensive standard library.

    - It was developed by Guido van Rossum.
- 1991: Visual Basic:
    - a third-generation event-driven programming language and integrated development environment (IDE) from Microsoft for its COM programming model.
- 1991: HTML (Hyper Text Mark-up Language):
    - It is the main markup language for preparing web pages and other information that can be displayed in a web browser.
- 1995: Java:
    - Java is a general-purpose, object-oriented and class-based programming language
    - It is intended to let application developers "write once, run anywhere" (WORA), meaning that code that runs on one platform does not need to be recompiled to run on another.
- 1995: JavaScript:
    - JavaScript (sometimes abbreviated as JS) is a scripting language commonly implemented as part of a web browser to create enhanced user interfaces and dynamic websites.
- 1995: PHP:
    - Hypertext Preprocessor was developed by Rasmus Lerdorf.
    - PHP is an open-source scripting language used for Web development to produce dynamic Web pages (server-side).
    - It is one of the first developed server-side scripting languages to be embedded into an HTML source document rather than calling an external file to process data.
- 2001: C#:
    - C Sharp is a multi-paradigm programming language
    - C sharp is an imperative, generic, object-oriented (class-based), and component-oriented programming language.
    - C sharp was developed by Microsoft within its .NET initiative.
- 2001: Visual Basic .NET:

    - It is an object-oriented computer programming language developed by Microsoft Inc. It can be viewed as an evolution of the classic Visual Basic (VB), implemented on the .NET Framework.
- 2011: Dart: Developed by Google, it's an open-source Web programming language.

4

Databases

Abstract

Biological databases that are composed of a large collection of digital nucleic acid sequences, protein sequences, or other polymer sequences stored on a computer, which is made available to the research community worldwide using web servers. The vast amount of information generated in molecular biology is analyzed, curated, tabulated, and arranged in databases. There are different types of biological databases, based on their contents. Besides, the database management system, a program to manage the databases, can be of two types: distributed DBMS and relational DBMS. This chapter briefly narrates the importance and purpose of biological databases.

Introduction

Biological databases are albums of biological data having meaningful relationship between them and organized in a tabular or flatfile form tha can be searched and retrieved by a computer or electeonic system. Some of the popular biological databases are GenBank (NCBI), Ensemble genomic database, Swiss-Prot (for protein sequences), Protein Databank (for protein structures). The first molecular database was made in 1965 by Margaret Dayhoff and her team at the National Biomedical Research Foundation (NBRF) for all protein sequences available at that time.

There are the following types of databases:

- **Primary databases:** these are the databases developed from the experimentally derived archival data. Primary databases include databases of nucleotide sequence, protein sequence, or macromolecular structure submitted directly into the database by researchers.
- **Secondary databases**: these are the curated data that have been derived from the results of analyzing primary data in the form of results of analysis, literature research, and interpretation.
- **Hybrid databases**: Many data resources have both primary and secondary characteristics.

Various important databases

	Database Short Name	Database Name
Sequence databases	DDBJ	DNA Data Bank of Japan (primary database)
	EMBL data	DNA primary database by European Bioinformatics Institute
	GenBank	GenBank nucleotide sequence database (primary database)
	CCDS	The Consensus CDS protein set database
	ENA	European Nucleotide Archive
	RefSeq	NCBI Reference Sequence Database
	UniGene	Database of computationally identifies transcripts from the same locus
	UniProtKB	Universal Protein Resource (UniProt) (primary database)
	InterPro	Proteins are classified into families InterPro predicts the presence of domains and sites
	OMIM	Online Mendelian Inheritance in Man
	PRINTS	A compendium of protein fingerprints
	neXtProt	A human protein-centric knowledge resource
	Pfam	Protein families database of alignments and HMMs
	PROSITE	Database of protein families and domains
	PIR	Protein Information Resource by Georgetown University Medical Center (primary database)
	NCBI	Protein and DNA sequence and knowledgebase by National Center for Biotechnology Information
	SUPERFAMILY	Library of HMMs representing superfamilies and database of (superfamily and family) annotations for all completely sequenced organisms
	Swiss-Prot	Protein knowledgebase (Swiss Institute of Bioinformatics) (primary database)
Structure databases	Protein Model Portal	Protein Model Portal of the PSI-Nature Structural Biology Knowledgebase
	SMR	Database of annotated 3D protein structure models
	DisProt	Database of Protein Disorder (database of experimental evidence of disorder in proteins)
	MobiDB	Database of intrinsically disordered and mobile proteins
	ModBase	Database of Comparative Protein Structure Models

	Database Short Name	Database Name
	PDBsum	Pictorial database of 3D structures in the Protein Data Bank
	PDB	Protein Data Bank for protein structure (primary database)
	SCOP	Structural Classification of Proteins
	CATH	Class, architecture, topology, and homologous superfamily
	SIMAP	Similarity Matrix of Proteins (SIMAP): a database of protein similarities computed using FASTA
	Swiss-model	Server and repository for protein structure models
	AAindex	Database of amino acid indices, amino acid mutation matrices, and pair-wise contact potentials
Protein-protein and other molecular interaction database	BioGRID	General repository for interaction datasets (Samuel Lunenfeld Research Institute)
	RBPDB	RNA-binding protein database
	IntAct	Open-source database for molecular interactions (EMBL-EBI)
	String	An open-source molecular interaction database to study interactions between proteins
	DIP	Database of Interacting Proteins (Univ. of California)
Expression databases	HPA	Human Protein Atlas: aims at mapping all the human proteins in cells, tissues, and organs
	GEO	Gene Expression Omnibus
	ArrayExpress	Any curated MIAME or MINSEQE-compliant transcriptomics data
Signal transduction pathway, Metabolic pathway, and protein function databases	PID	NCI-Nature Pathway Interaction Database
	Netpath	Curated resource of signal transduction pathways in humans
	Reactome	Navigable map of human biological pathways, ranging from metabolic processes to hormonal signaling
	WikiPathways	Database for biological pathways
	SABIO-RK	Database for biochemical reactions and their kinetic properties

	Database Short Name	Database Name
	BioCyc	Database Collection includes EcoCyc and MetaCyc
	BRENDA	The comprehensive enzyme information system, including FRENDA, AMENDA, DRENDA, and KENDA
	HMDB	Contains detailed information about small molecule metabolites found in the human body
	KEGG	KEGG PATHWAY Database (Univ. of Kyoto)
	MANET	Molecular ancestry network database
Taxonomic databases	BacDive	Bacterial metadatabase that provides strain-linked information about bacterial and archaeal biodiversity, including taxonomy information
	Catalogue of Life	A meta-database of all species on earth
	EzTaxon-e	Database for the identification of prokaryotes based on 16S ribosomal RNA gene sequences
	NCBI Taxonomy	A taxonomic database operated by NCBI and concentrating on all taxa for which DNA sequences are available
Meta databases	ConsensusPathDB:	A molecular functional interaction database, integrating information from 12 others
	Entrez	National Center for Biotechnology Information
	Neuroscience Information Framework	Integrates hundreds of neuroscience-relevant resources

Sequence search against sequence databases

A sequence database involves searching for similarities between genomic/protein sequences and a query sequence to find the best match sequences based on threshold criteria. The number of matches/hits is used to formulate a score that determines the similarity between the sequence query and the sequences in the sequence database.

5

Sequence Alignment

Abstract

Sequence alignment is the positioning of DNA, RNA, or protein sequences with each other to identify the regions of identity, which may be the result of functional, structural, or evolutionary relationships between the sequences. Therefore, sequence alignment is the process of aligning two sequences to achieve the maximum levels of identity and conservation. This chapter deals with the basic concept of sequence alignment and the tools associated with multiple sequence alignment. Further, it describes various matrices used in sequence alignment.

Introduction

Sequence alignment compares the homologous sequences for the residues and puts the similar residues column-wise so that we can understand the degree of similarity and divergence among the sequences. One important terminology associated with molecular sequence alignment is substitution matrix. It contains the values proportional to the probability that amino acid "i" mutates to amino acid "j" for all pairs of amino acids. Early matrices used for sequence alignment are unitary scoring matrix; minimum mutation distance matrix and matrix based on physical, chemical, and structural properties.

Types of sequence alignment

1. Pairwise Sequence Alignment

To find similarities between two biological sequences that may indicate functional, structural, and/or evolutionary relationships (protein or nucleic acid). Methods for finding the best-matching pairwise (local or global) alignments of two query sequences are used in pairwise sequence alignment methods. Pairwise alignments can only be used between two sequences at a time, but they are fast to compute and are frequently used for methods that do not require extreme precision.

Methods for Pairwise Sequence Alignment

Dot-matrix methods: The dot-matrix method, which generates a family of alignments for individual sequence regions, is qualitative and conceptually simple, but time-consuming to analyze on a large scale. Certain sequence features, such as insertions, deletions, repeats, or inverted repeats, can be easily identified visually from a dot-matrix plot in the absence of noise.

Dynamic programming: provides the very best or optimal alignment between sequences. Both global and local alignments can be done by simple changes in the basic dynamic programming algorithm.

- **Global alignments**: attempt to align every residue in both the sequences, and are most useful when the sequences in the query set are similar and of roughly equal size. However, global alignments can start and/ or end in gaps. Eg. Needleman–Wunsch algorithm is based on dynamic programming by proposed Needleman and Wunsch (1970). Here, 1 is awarded for the match and 0 for the mismatch.
- **Local alignments**: useful for dissimilar sequences, which contain regions of similarity. Eg. Smith–Waterman algorithm is based on the same dynamic programming with additional choices to start and end at any place, proposed by Temple Smith and Mike Waterman (1981). It initializes the edges of the Matrix as 0.
- **Quasi Global alignment**: enters a shorter sequence within the best matching region of a longer sequence. Eg. Sellers D.P.

Word methods: Word methods, also known as *k-tuple* methods, are heuristic methods that are significantly more efficient than dynamic programming but do not guarantee finding an optimal alignment solution, but are very fast.

Word methods extract a series of short, nonoverlapping subsequences ("words") from the query sequence, which are then matched to candidate database sequences. The word method is best known for its use in the database search tools in FASTA and BLAST (Basic Local Alignment Search Tool).

2. Multiple Sequence Alignment

When three or more related sequences are aligned so that the greatest number of similar characters is aligned in the same column of the alignment. MSA is done to identify conserved sequences, determine consensus sequences, and evolutionary analyses (selection pressure, pair-wise distance), MSA is a prerequisite for phylogenetic analysis for many of the phylogenetic algorithms. Besides, MSA is used to predict the secondary and tertiary structures of new sequences, prediction of functionality, design degenerate primers of PCR, etc.

Methods for Multiple Sequence Alignment

Progressive methods: is one of the fastest and most efficient, based on a heuristic approach. This is accomplished by constructing a series of pairwise alignments. At first, two sequences are selected and aligned using standard pairwise alignment; this alignment is fixed. Then, a third sequence is chosen and aligned to the first alignment, and so on until all sequences have been aligned.

Motif finding: also known as profile analysis, builds global multiple sequence alignments that attempt to align short conserved sequence motifs among the query set's sequences. Highly conserved regions are identified and used to build a set of profile matrices.

ClustalW is a general-purpose multiple alignment program for amino acid or nucleotide sequences. ClustalW is produced by Julie D. Thompson and Toby Gibson of the European Molecular Biology Laboratory, Germany, and Desmond Higgins of the European Bioinformatics Institute, Cambridge, UK. Here "W" stands for weight. ClustalX is the downloadable, offline version of ClustalW.

Structural alignment: When, sequences have very low sequence similarity (<20%), then in place of sequences, structure alignment is performed. It is specific to protein sequences but can also be used for RNA sequences, using information about the secondary and tertiary structure of the protein or RNA molecule to help align the sequences.

These methods can be applied to two or more sequences and typically produce local alignments; however, because they rely on the availability of structural information, they can only be applied to sequences with known corresponding structures (usually through X-ray crystallography or NMR spectroscopy). In evaluating alignments for homology-based protein structure prediction structure alignments are employed.

- **Gap-penalty**: During sequence alignment, to compensate for the insertion or deletion of query sequences, gaps in the sequences are introduced. The introduction or extension of a gap is penalized in the scoring of an alignment of nucleotide or protein sequences called the gap penalty.
- **Scoring Matrices**: A set of values for quantifying the likelihood of one residue substituted by another in an alignment. An amino-acid scoring matrix is a 20x20 table with positions indexed with amino acids, such that position X, and Y in the table gives the score for aligning amino-acid X with amino acid Y.

Substitutation matrices

The scoring system is called Substitutation matrices which comprise scores for residue identity, substitution, and insertions or deletions.

Two popular empirical scoring models for protein sequences are PAM and BLOSUM.

Percent Accepted Mutation (PAM)

Percent Accepted Mutation or Dayhoff matrix or Mutation Data Matrix is derived from an evolutionary model where **all positions are equally mutable.** It is based on a specific set of observations of mutational frequency. The entries describe the **probabilities of each residue to be mutated** to the corresponding residue. 1 PAM= 1 residue out of 100 undergoes mutation and 1 PAM corresponds to the average change in 1% of all amino acid positions. More distantly related proteins can arise by a series of uncorrelated mutations that can be described by the PAM matrix. The number signifies evolutionary distances (greater number means greater distance): PAM N matrix= N% PAM= N x PAM1. Thus, **100 PAM** is not necessary that all residue will mutate and homologous proteins are separated by more than 100 PAM. The limitation of the PAM matrix is that there is no general correspondence between the PAM distance and evolutionary times, as different proteins evolved at different times.

BLOSUM Family of Matrices

The Blocks Amino Acid Substitution matrix (BLOSUM) values are based on observed amino acid substitution of appx. 2000 conserved amino acids (Blocks) from 500 families of related proteins, given by Steven Henikoff and Jorja G. Henikoff (1992). In each block, all sequences that share at least x% identity are grouped to yield BLOSUM x. The **merit of BLOSUM** is that it is based on observed alignments, not extrapolated from comparisons of closely related proteins and the limitation is that it yields no evolutionary models. BLOSUM 62 is often a default matrix in several search programs. The features are derived from distantly related evolutionary local ungapped sequences. Please note that BLOSUM 62 is the default matrix of BLAST 2.0.

Relationship between PAM and BLOSUM Matrices

- For single database search, the BLOSUM matrix generally performs better
- The BLOSUM matrix is based on the replacement pattern found in the highly conserved regions of the sequence

- PAM matrix contains relatively fewer data– C to W mutation is not mentioned

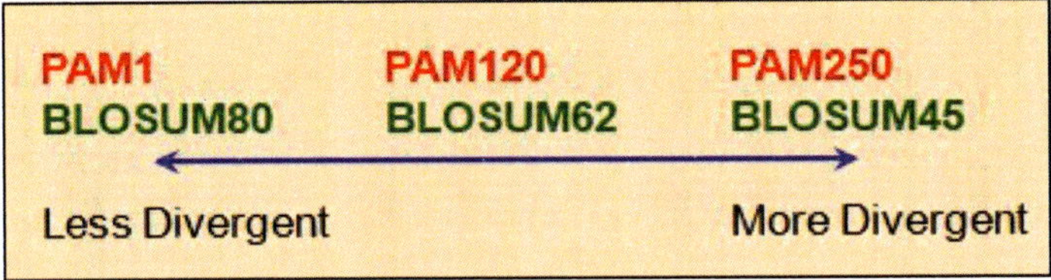

Domain analysis

Protein domains are critical for understanding a protein's molecular function. A protein domain is a structurally and functionally conserved portion of a protein sequence. A protein domain typically has a length of 25 to 500 amino acids. The entire protein sequence is not required for some protein domain analyses.

6

Molecular Phylogeny

Abstract

Molecular phylogeny is an important method for understanding the evolutionary relationships between different organisms. Molecular phylogeny is based on the idea that organisms that share a more recent common ancestor will have more similarities in their DNA or protein sequences. The chapter seems to cover the basic concepts and terminology used in molecular phylogeny, including the difference between rooted and unrooted trees, as well as various methods used for constructing phylogenetic trees. Further, chapter also covers some common tools and software used for analyzing molecular data and constructing phylogenetic trees. Overall, this chapter provides a useful introduction to molecular phylogeny and the methods used for understanding the evolutionary relationships between different organisms. Understanding these concepts is important for many areas of biological research, including evolutionary biology, ecology, and biotechnology.

Introduction

The evolutionary history of a species is constructed in a form of a tree using molecular sequence data. The principle behind molecular phylogenetic tree construction is exploring the relatedness among various organisms due to descending from a nearer or remote common ancestor (CA). There are various methods of phylogenetic tree construction, using molecular sequences or distance data between the species/strains, etc. There are some important terminologies used in molecular phylogeny which are required to be defined first.

Terminologies used in molecular phylogeny (Mukhopadhyay et al., 2017)

- **Clade**: a group of individuals that have originated from a single clan. Thus, clad refers to mono-phyletic DNA sequences designating an ancestral lineage comprising of the ancestor and all descendants of the ancestor.

- **Branch length**: The total number of changes (in sequence) between two leaves is the sum of the branch lengths between the two leaves through the in between common ancestor(s). The branch length is thus proportional to evolutionary distance determined by the number of substitution per site.
- **Distance scale**: scale representing the number of differences between the input sequences used in phylogenetic analysis. If the scale is a fractiuon between 0 to 1, the value may be multiplied with 100 to indicate the differences in percentage.
- **Dendrogram**: is a broad generalized term that represents a phylogenetic tree. This generic term is applied to any scaled or unscaled of phylogenetic tree.
- **Cladogram**: It is a branching tree that denotes the relatedness of the leaves with the common ancestor. However, the branch-length is not proportrional to the genetic change or distance between the OTUs. A clade simply means a common ancestor and the descendants (here, species) of that common ancestor.
- **Unrooted Tree**: Unrooted tree depicts the degree of relkatedness between the OTUs, although the ancestry is not indicated by it.
- **Rooted Tree**: On th ecotrary, a rooted tree is a directed tree that depicts the unique common ancestor(s) of the OTUs.
- **Operational taxonomic unit (OTU)**: Robert Sokal and Peter H coined this term in 1963 to refer to any group of organisms that are distinct from each other and are being used for taxonomic or evolutionary or phylogenetic analyses. Molecular phylogenetic analysis using 16s rRNA bins the similar sequences of bacteria into OUT to indicate the siomaler sequences as Unit.
- **Molecular Clock**: represents a constant pace of the evolutionary process. It is represented by a phylogenetic distance-preserving tree that can be presented along a time axis. Each node is assigned the time during which it has evolved
- **Phylograms** are the diagrammatic representations of molecular phylogeny that has been constructed through statistical analysis of the molecular data (DNA/RNA/Peptide sequences). The branch length of phylograms indicates the degree of evolutionary change of the taxa.
- **Chronograms** are cladograms with time scale, where the branch length is proportional to the time scale (generally in million years).

- **The molecular clock** is constructed with the assumption of specific mutation rate, based on which the time of divergence during the process of is calculated.

Methods used in molecular phylogeny

- **Unweighted pair group method with arithmetic mean (UPGMA)**: This is a distance based method that is based on agglomerative hierarchical clustering. It is one of the simplest method to construct phylogenetic tree with the assumptions of constant rate of evolution and simultaneous sampling of all input sequences, which are not much realistic. Hence, the practicality of the inferred tree is compromised. The tree assumes molecular clock hypothesis (hence, ultrametric) and the scale bar indicates additive evolutionary distance. The additive property of branching pattern of a tree means the summation of the lengths of the branches connecting two taxa commensurate to the distance between the taxa. All the terminal taxa are equally distant from the root.
- **Neighbor-joining (NJ)**: It is a distance-based method that makes use of a greedy algorithm that attempts to construct a tree with minimal sum of all the branch lengths. It also assumes additive property of branch lengths. The assumption of different evolution rate is also considered, thereby rejecting the assumption of molecular clock. The NJ and minimum evolution trees share a similarity while using non-ultrametric distance data and exploiting the additivity feature of branch lengths. The algorithm of NJ tree construction works on principle of clustering.

    1. **Maximum Parsimony Method**: It is a character-based method (not distance-based) to generate a phylogenetic tree through evaluating the possible evolutionary relationships among the OTUs, so that the most parsimonious relationship is selected and the number of evolutionary steps is minimized. The simplest or the most parsimonious option creates a multiple sequence alignment that can identify which columns reveal the maximum information about the evolution. The term parsimonious emphasizes on the minimum number of changes needed to explain the sequence data. Here, the number of substitutions between the sequence pairs is done. The scale bar is not the representative of genetic distance or time. Re-sampling method like bootstrap is used to show the agreement of branching of the the consensus tree. The scale bar refers to either the proportion of nucleotide substitution per site or nucleotide substitution per unit length.

2. **Minimum Evolution (ME)**: It is also a distance-based method and like NJ method, it assumes minimum number of evolutionary event. In many instances, an ME tree works on the principle of minimum total length of its branches. Although, this feature is not mandatory for all cases, particularly when the input sequences are of short length. The similarity between ME and maximum parsimony methods is the feature of "minimum number of evolutionary event", however, they differ in terms of the source data (ME is distance based method (like, UPGMA, NJ) but MP is character based method like Maximum likelihood and Bayesian method).
3. **Maximum likelihood (ML)**: It is the best and most robust method when divenrgent sequences are used for tree construction. ML makes use of both distance and character information from the input sequences. It was developed by Felsenstein in 1981. The probabilities of the nodal connections are calculated through the evolutionary model to construct the tree and assigning branch lengths.

7

Primer Designing

Abstract

PCR primer design is a crucial skill for molecular biologists, as it enables the study of gene expression, gene amplification, and molecular markers. Primer3 is an online tool widely used for designing optimal PCR primers, which are pairs of short oligonucleotides that initiate DNA synthesis in vitro using a thermocycler. This tool uses a range of parameters to generate high-quality primers, including target sequence length, melting temperature, GC content, specificity, and product size. Understanding and effectively utilizing these parameters is essential for achieving accurate and reliable PCR results. In this chapter, the practical aspect of primer designing using the online tool Primer3 has been discussed. The parameters and the purpose of their usage have been given in a tabulated manner.

Introduction

A primer is a short synthetic oligonucleotide, used to initiate PCR amplification in each cycle. Amplicon refers to the gene-specific nucleotide sequences amplified by PCR. The term **Gibb's free energy** is important in primer designing. The Gibbs free energy of a system at any time is defined as the enthalpy (H) of the system - the product of the entropy (S) of the system times the temperature (T) i.e. G=H-ST.

- **Analyzing Gibbs free energy (Delta G)**: The "Gibbs Free Energy" (ΔG), in a generalized term, is a measure of the quantity of work yielded by a system that is operational at a steady pressure. Lowering the value (considering the + or - symbol) indicates the spontaneity of the reaction. So, $\Delta G = -6$ signifies that the oligo and the template will more spontaneously anneal than the other oligo exhibiting $\Delta G = -3$ kcal/mol. We can use the online tool "IDT Oligo Analyzer" (http://eu.idtdna.com/analyzer/applications/oligoanalyzer/) for calculating ΔG values of the oligos.

Primer designing using Primer-3 online tool

a. Open Primer 3 online tool: https://bioinfo.ut.ee/primer3-0.4.0/

b. Paste the sequence

c. Specify the parameters (please see the table: "Parameters to consider during primer designing", below)

d. Verify the primers using IDT oligo-analyzer: https://sg.idtdna.com/site/account

e. Select the based primers

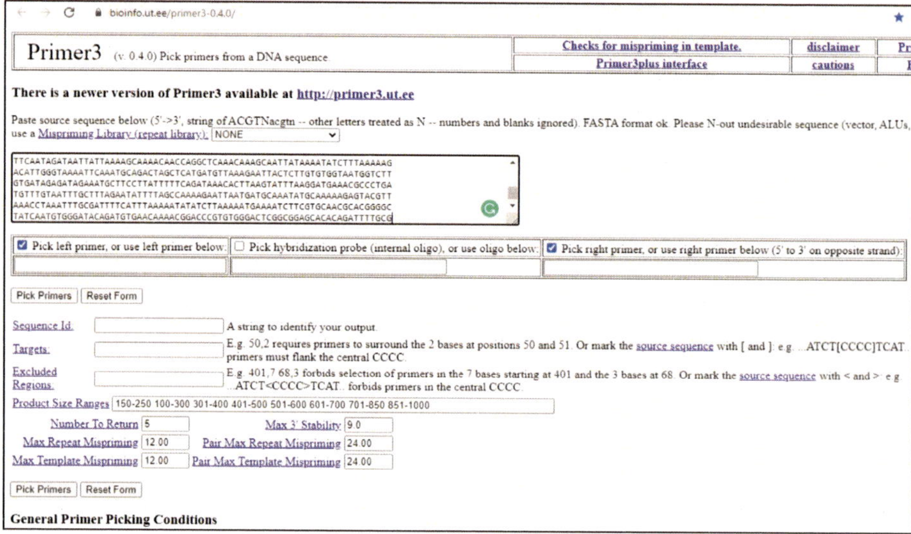

Acceptable values of ΔG for various secondary structures of oligos

S.N	Secondary structures	Acceptable ΔG
1	3'-end hairpin	> -2 kcal/mol
2	Internal hairpin	> -3 kcal/mol
3	3'-end self-dimer	> -5 kcal/mol
4	Internal self-dimers	> -6 kcal/mol
5	3'-end cross-dimer	> -5 kcal/mol
6	Internal cross-dimer	> -6 kcal/mol
7	5 bases from the 3'-end of primers	>= -9 Kcal/mol

Parameters to consider during primer designing (Mukhopadhyay et al., 2017)

S.N	Feature	Ideal value or range	Discussion
1		• 18-25 nucleotide (nt)	The length of the oligo determines the fate of the PCR: • Short primers (8-10 bases) exhibit low specificity; • Very long primers (>25 bases): has compromised efficacy to anneal to template, which could be attributed to the formation of secondary structures • Long primers need more time to anneal and denature • Primers for multiplexing: are very long (30 to 35 bp) • Primers for random priming (viz. RAPD): are short like, Octamers to tri-decamer
2	*Melting temperature (T_m)*	• Two primers may differ in T_m by 1-2 °C . • Average annealing temperature is 5°C less than the average T_m of the primer-pair • *Optimal T_m* 52°C - 62°C	• T_m of an oligo is defined as the sepcific temperature at which half of the primer is hybridized with the template. • T_m below 45°C could encourage secondary annealing and spurious amplification. If T_m>65-70°C of the primers for automated sequencing, secondary priming artifacts, and noisy amplicons are evident. • Higher T_m (75°C to 80°C) is recommended for amplifying the high G/C content of targets
3	*Primer G/C content*	• Optimum is 45-55%	• GC percentage can vary between 40-60% • GC-centent also determines the annealing temperature of the primers
4	*G/C Clamp*	• 2 G/C within the last four bases at 3' end of the primer	• 3 or more G/C clamps could make the primer 'sticky' due to higher T_m at the 3' terminus • 3'-terminus of the primer is crucial. G/C at 3'-end increases the efficiency of the primers.
5	*Stretches of nucleotides*	• Max. of 4 dinucleotides or 4 mono-nucleotide repeats in a primer	• Runs of the same bases increase the probability of primer-dimer and hairpin loop formation • This could lead to the annealing of primer(s) to an unintended template due to chance similarity between complementary sequences that lead to low Gibb's free energy at the 3'-end

S.N	Feature	Ideal value or range	Discussion
6	*Optimal amplicon size*	• SSCP: < 400 bases; Cloning: 200- several kbs; • Real-time- qPCR: 80-200 bp; • RFLP studies: amplicon length varies	• qPCR: the amplicon size is generally between 90 to 200 bases • The amplicon length is determined by the purpose of the experiment, rather than the rules for designing "good" primers
7.	*Cross homology* • No cross-homology is recommended in the genome of a species	• Cross-homology will result in mispriming • Do Primer-BLAST to check possible spurious amplifications.	• Exon-exon junctions of complementary DNA strands ought to be targeted to amplify mRNA/ cDNA to prevent genomic DNA from amplification during PCR.

8

Primer Designing for qPCR (SYBR Green Chemistry)

Abstract

Real-time PCR, also known as qPCR, is a highly sensitive technique used to determine the real-time amplification of a target DNA sequence. However, the presence of secondary structures or spurious amplicons can distort the results. When using SYBR Green chemistry, the features of qPCR primers differ from those of standard endpoint PCR primers. As a result, designing primers for SYBR Green qPCR requires extra caution and attention. This chapter outlines the essential features and conditions for designing qPCR primers, including primer length, melting temperature, GC content, specificity, and avoiding primer-dimer formation.

Introduction

The real-time PCR is methodically different from end-point PCR. The primers of qPCR primers are required to be very specific with highly reproducible results under similar conditions. The amplicon length is also limited (varies between 90 to 200 bp) so that the fluorescence can be precisely detected and also differentiated from primer-dimers, if any.

This chapter will highlight the features of qPCR primers (for SYBR Green chemistry) in the following section.

Optimal and permissible ranges of parameters of qPCR primers (SYBR green chemistry) (Mukhopadhyay et al., 2017)

S.N	Feature	Optimal	Limits	Comments
1	Length of each primer	21-23 nt	18-25 nt	Shorter primers could increase mispriming and longer primers would reduce efficiency
2	Amplicon length	90-200 bp	80-220 bp	Primers for qPCR using chemistry other than SYBR Green uses shorter amplicon (60-150 bp)
3	Primer Tm	65°C	58-68°C	The difference between the Tm of 2 primers should not be more than 2°C
4	Annealing Temperature	60°C	57-64°C	The annealing and extension temperature of the Taq is recommended to be the same
5	GC% of Primer	55-65%	35-80%	Higher or lower GC% would affect the Tm of primers
6	GC-clamp at 3'- end	1 clamp	Max. 2 clamps	More than 2 G/C clamps with the last five bases at 3'-end will make the primers sticky
7	Run of identical bases	2 bases	Maximum 4	Identical bases or dinucleotide runs increases the likelihood of secondary structure formation
8	3'-end stability of primers	Delta G >= -9 Kcal/mol	Minus 7 to -11 Kcal/mol	Delta G of the last five bases at 3'-end should be more (ignoring the symbol) than that of the internal region of the primer
9	Max Repeat Mispriming	12 or more	11 to 15	A larger value inversely proportionates the probability of repeat mispriming of the primers
10	The proportion of different bases	An equal percentage of each base	Minimum 20-30% of one base	

9

Basic Local Alignment Search Tool (BLAST)

Abstract

The Basic Local Alignment Search Tool, or BLAST, is an online tool provided by the National Center for Biotechnology Information (NCBI) that allows users to search for matches between their query sequences and the sequences stored in NCBI databases. BLAST can be used to search for nucleotide sequences against nucleotide sequences, protein sequences against protein sequences, and protein sequences against translated nucleotide sequences in the databases. BLAST is widely used to study sequence similarity, identify target sequences, analyze the functional aspects of molecular sequences, and investigate evolutionary relationships. This chapter details on the BLAST and its applications.

Introduction

BLAST enables to the comparison of a query sequence with the whole library or database of sequences very fast and identifies database sequences that resemble below a certain threshold E-Value. Given below is the screenshot of the homepage of NCBI BLAST (https://blast.ncbi.nlm.nih.gov/Blast.cgi).

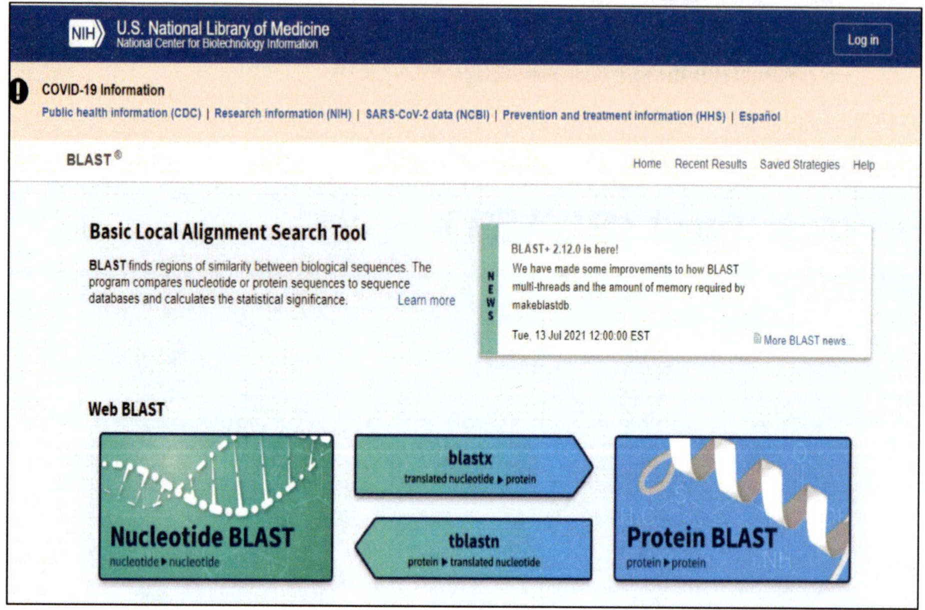

Types of BLAST algorithms

BLASTn	The term BLASTn stands for standard Nucleotide BLAST. Here, two nucleotide sequences are compared. Word BLAST stands for Basic Local Alignment Search Tool, which is an online software to compare query sequences from an online available database.
BLASTp	The term BLASTn stands for protein BLAST. Here two amino acid sequences are aligned and compared.
BLASTx	BLASTx aligns six conceptually translated DNA sequences from both stands with a database of protein sequences.
tBLASTn	Alignment of protein vs. translated nucleotide sequences for the identification of database sequences that encode proteins.
tBLASTx	Alignment of translated nucleotide vs. translated nucleotide sequences for identification of nucleotide sequences based on their coding potential.

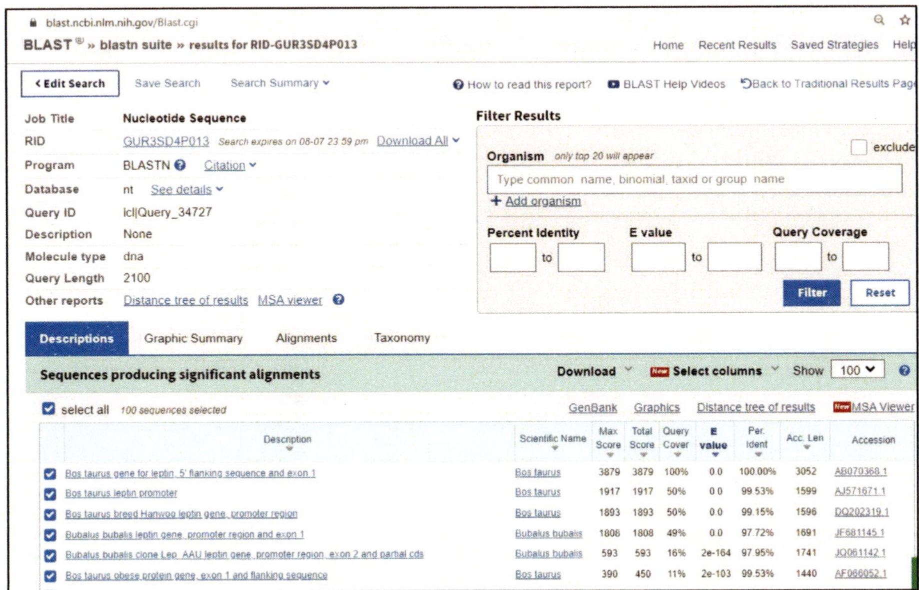

Result of BLASTn analysis of bovine leptin gene sequence

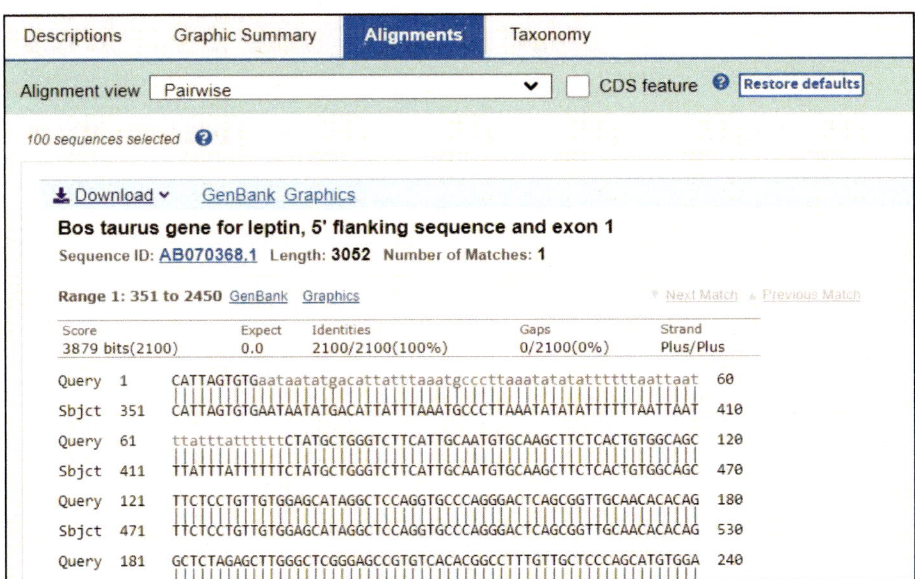

The following terms are associated with Protein BLAST (BLASTp)

- *Position Hit Initiated BLAST (PHI-BLAST)*: A variant of PSI-BLAST, based on the construction of a Position-Specific Scoring Matrix (PSSM) around a motif of protein.

- *Position-Specific Iterative BLAST (PSI-BLAST)*: PSI-BLAST is an iterative search of the protein BLAST algorithm.
- *Position-Specific Scoring Matrix (PSSM)*: PSSM is a profile providing matching of an amino acid of a target sequence from a query sequence, estimated by log-odd scores.

10

Fasta

Abstract

FASTA, which stands for "Fast All", is a sequence alignment tool developed by William R. Pearson and David J. Lipman in 1985. It is commonly used to identify similarities between DNA and protein sequences. FASTA employs a "hashing" strategy to locate matches for short stretches of identical residues with a length of k, referred to as k-tuples or k-tups. This method enables FASTA to quickly search large databases for sequence similarities, making it a popular tool for identifying homologous sequences, predicting gene functions, and analyzing evolutionary relationships. This chapter elaborates some basics of FASTA.

Introduction

A k-tup is composed of 2 residues for protein sequences and 6 residues for DNA sequences. Thus, the query sequence is broken down into sequence patterns or words known as k-tuples, and the target sequences are searched for these k-tuples to find similarities between the two.

FASTA is a fast homology search tool. Although these methods do not guarantee optimal alignment or true homologs, they are 50 to 100 times faster than dynamic programming.

The types of FASTA programs are given below

- TFASTA : Compares a query protein sequence to a protein library or DNA sequence to a DNA library.
- FASTS : Compares a set of short peptide fragments, as would be obtained from mass-spec. analysis of a protein, against a protein (fasts) or DNA (tfasts) database.
- FASTX and Y: Compares a DNA sequence to a protein sequence database, translating it in three forward (or reverse) frames and allowing for frameshifts.

- LALIGN/PLALIGN: Compares two protein sequences to find sequence similarities.
- LALIGN can identify similarities due to internal repeats or similar regions that cannot be aligned by FASTA because of gaps, it reports sequence alignments and similarity scores.
- PLALIGN plots out a graph of the sequence alignments, which looks much like a "dot-plot".

Parameters used in the FASTA algorithm

Threshold: It is a boundary of minimum or maximum value which can be used to filter out words during comparison.

True Homology: In FASTA true homology refers to how much the sequence is similar to the query sequence.

E-value: It decreases exponentially with the score that is assigned to an alignment between two sequences. E values below 10-6 are considered the most statistically significant. E values above 10-6 but below 10-3 deserve a second look. E values above 10-3 should be thrown out with great force.

Putative conserved domains: These are the domains that have different functionalities.

FASTA format description: A sequence in FASTA format consists of one line starting with a ">" sign, followed by a sequence identification code.

It is optionally followed by a textual description of the sequence. Since it is not part of the official description of the format, software can choose to ignore this, when it is present. One or more lines containing the sequence itself. A file in FASTA format may comprise more than one sequence.

The FASTA format is sometimes also referred to as the "Pearson" format (after the author of the FASTA program and format).

>crab_anapl ALPHA CRYSTALLIN B CHAIN (ALPHA(B)-CRYSTALLIN).

MDITIHNPLIRRPLFSWLAPSRIFDQIFGEHLQESELLPASPSLSPFLMR

SPIFRMPSWLETGLSEMRLEKDKFSVNLDVKHFSPEELKVKVLGD
M V E I H G K H E E R Q D E H G F I A R E F N R K Y R I P A D
VDPLTITSSLSLDGVLTVSAPRKQSDVPERSIPITREEKPAIAGAQRK

Source: https://www.bioinformatics.nl/tools/crab_fasta.html

11

Omics

Abstract

Omics arise from ome which means complete or totality. It refers to the collection of technologies used to investigate the roles, relationships, and actions of the various types of molecules that make up an organism's cells. Omics technologies provide the tools required to investigate differences in DNA, RNA, proteins, and other cellular molecules between species and individuals within a species. These technologies comprise, genomics, transcriptomics, proteomics, metabolomics, ionomics, glycomics, lipomics, cultureomics, pharmacogenomics, metagenomics, foodomics, eigenomics, phenomics, etc. The inclusion of all omics domain is known as multiomics. In this chapter we describe from basic, type structure of omics to all the recent cutting edge technologies in multiomics.

Genome: Coined by Hans Winkler in 1920 to define the complete set of genetic information in an organism.

Genomics: Study of the structure and function of the entire genome of a living organism is known as Genomics. The term was coined by Thomas Roderick in 1986.

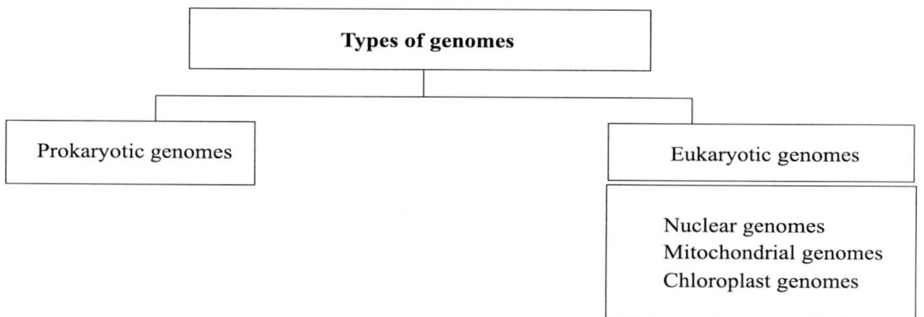

Important signal sequences found in prokaryotes and eukaryotes

S.N.	Sequence name	Sequence (5'-3')*	Purpose
1	*Prinbow box or "-10 Box"*	TAT AAT	In prokaryotes, during transcription, the AT-rich (-10 box) partially dissociates following the formation of a closed promoter complex.
2	*"-35 Box"*	TTG ACA T	In prokaryotes, the σ subunit of the RNA polymerase recognizes and binds the -35 box of the promoter to produce a closed promoter complex during the initiation of transcription.
3	*TATA Box or "-25 Box" or Goldberg Hogness Box*	TATA(A/T)A(A/T)	In eukaryotes, the TATA box in the promoter acts as the attachment site for RNA polymerase-II with the help of some transcription factors.
4	*CAT Box or "-90 Box"*	GGC CAA TAT	It is a eukaryotic promoter element that acts as a binding site for transcription factors to stimulate or repress transcription initiation.
5	*GC Box*	GGG CGG	In eukaryotes, for the genes lacking the TATA box the GC box, located -10 to 20 bp (i.e. upstream of the start codon) acts as the binding site for the transcription factor.
6	*5' splicing signal sequence*	AGG TAA GT	It is the 5' signal sequence in pre-mRNA for splicing.
7	*3' splicing signal sequence*	Y_6NCAG	It is the 3' signal sequence in pre-mRNA.
8	*Branchpoint lariat sequence*	CURAY	In vertebrates (in Yeast the sequence is "5'-UACUAAC-3") this sequence is present in 10 to 40 bases upstream of the 3' splice site sequence that participates in lariat formation during splicing of pre-mRNA.
9	*Polyadenylation signal sequence*	AAU AAA	It dictates the polyadenylation of pre-mRNA with the help of poly(A) polymerase enzyme.
10	*Shine Dalgarno sequence*	AGG AGG U	In prokaryotes, the small ribosomal subunit binds to this sequence before the initiation of translation.
11	*Telomeric non-coding sequence*	TTA GGG	The repeat sequence in the leading strand of telomere (in human) partially bind to the RNA molecule present in the telomerase.

Why sequence genomes?

- Determining the order of nucleotide bases.
- Position of every gene, chromosome order, and the coding sequence that determines the function of each gene.
- Allow us to compare the DNA of closely related species to establish and analyze their genetic differences.
- Haemophilus influenzae was the first organism to have its entire genome sequenced in 1995.

Evolution of sequencing technologies

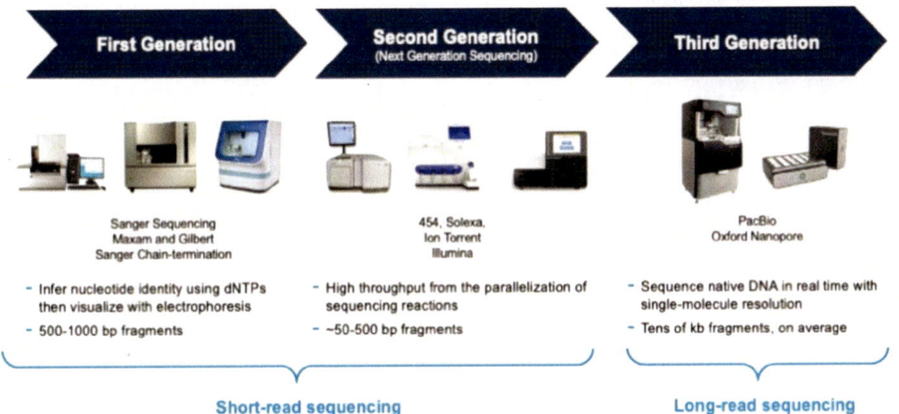

Subfields of genomics

1. **Structural genomics:** To characterize the structure of the genome.
2. **Functional genomics:** Functions of genes and non-gene sequences in genomes. Aims to collect and use sequencing data for describing gene and protein functions.
3. **Comparative genomics:** Aims to compare genomic features between different species.
4. **Mutational genomics:** Aims to identify mutations in and across the genomes of the species.
   - **NGS:** NGS stands for next-generation sequencing, which is a massively parallel sequencing technique that provides ultra-high throughput, scalability, and speed. The technology is used to determine the nucleotide order in entire genomes or specific DNA

or RNA regions. NGS has revolutionized biology, allowing labs to perform a wide range of applications and study biological systems at a level never before possible.

- **Indels:** insertions and deletions.
- **CNVs:** copy number variations.
- **SNPs:** Single nucleotide polymorphisms (SNPs), are the most common type of genetic variation among people. They are usually bi-allelic.
- **SNP genotyping chip:** The measurement of genetic variations of SNPs between members of a species is known as SNP genotyping. It's a type of genotyping SNP chip or array, which is the study of a larger range of genetic variation.
- **HapMap:** It is known as the Map of Genetic Variation, HapMap Project is to determine the common patterns of DNA sequence variation in any genome.
- **ENCODE project**: Launched by the National Human Genome Research Institute and aims to identify and characterize all the genes in the human genome.
- **SCG:** Single-cell genomics.

Transcriptomics: Transcriptomics is the study of the transcriptome i.e. the entire set of transcript (including all coding and non-coding RNAs) molecules expressed in some given entity, such as a cell, tissue, or organism, the term was coined by Charles Auffray (Pietu et al., 1999).

Various techniques to analyze transcriptome

- **ESTs:** Expressed sequence tags (ESTs) are a single RNA transcript that generates a short nucleotide sequence. Before being sequenced, RNA is first copied as complementary DNA (cDNA) by a reverse transcriptase enzyme.
- **SAGE:** Serial analysis of gene expression (SAGE)
- **CAGE:** cap analysis gene expression
- **Microarrays:** are made up of short nucleotide oligomers called "probes" that are arranged in a grid on a glass slide. Its goal is to detect the expression of thousands of genes in a sample at the same time. It is based on the photolithography technique.

- **RNA-Seq:** analyses the constantly changing cellular transcriptome to reveal the presence and quantity of RNA in a biological sample at any given time. RNA-Seq also allows for a much more precise measurement of transcript levels and isoforms than other methods.
- **SCT:** Single-Cell Transcriptomics (SCT) enables gene expression to be dissected at single-cell resolution, revolutionizing transcriptomic research. Methods such as 10X Chromium can profile millions of cells in parallel, generating a large amount of data.

Some important terminologies

Cultureomics: is the high-throughput cell culture of bacteria to identify strains or species in samples obtained from tissues such as the human gut or the environment. It is an alternative, complementary method to metagenomics.

Epigenomics: is the investigation of all epigenetic changes in a cell. Changes in the way genes are turned on and off without changing the DNA sequence are referred to as epigenetic changes. They can be caused by aging and environmental factors such as diet, exercise, drugs, and chemicals. Epigenetic changes can influence a person's disease risk and can be passed down from parents to children.

Foodomics: is a comprehensive, high-throughput approach to utilizing food science in the context of improving human nutrition. It is a new approach to food and nutrition that studies the food domain as a whole in conjunction with the nutrition domain to achieve the main goal of optimizing human health and well-being.

Glycomics: aim to identify the entire repertoire of glycans produced by a cell or tissue under a specific time, location, and environmental conditions.

Glycoproteomics: determines which sites on each glycoprotein of a cell are glycosylated and, ideally, includes the identification and quantification of each glycan structure at each site on the cell's heterogeneous glycoforms.

Interactomics: deals with the study of the interactome.

Ionomics: is the quantitative measurement of the entire set of ions in a living organism, and it deals with changes in ion production in response to various external stimuli.

Lipomics: is the comprehensive study of the production of lipids.

Metabolomics: is the large-scale study of small molecules known as metabolites found in cells, biofluids, tissues, or organisms. The metabolome refers to these small molecules and their interactions within a biological system as a whole.

Metagenomics: the study of the metagenome, the collective genome of microorganisms from an environmental sample to provide information on the microbial diversity and ecology of a particular environment is known as metagenomics.

Pharmacogenomic: is an investigation of how a person's genes influence how they react to medications. Its long-term goal is to assist doctors in selecting the drugs and dosages that are best suited for each individual. It falls under the purview of precision medicine, which seeks to treat each patient on an individual basis.

Phenomics: is the collection of high-dimensional phenotypic data on an organism-wide scale. It was coined by UC Berkeley and LBNL scientist Steven A. Garan. Phenomics concepts are employed in functional genomics, pharmaceutical research, metabolic engineering, agricultural research, and in phylogenetics.

Proteogenomics: is a field of study that combines proteomics and genomics resulted in the emergence of proteogenomics as a separate field in 2004.

Proteome: is an organism's entire set of proteins that are produced or modified. The word proteome is a combination of protein and genome and was coined by Mark Wilkins in 1994.

Proteomics: the study of proteins on a large scale.

12

Protein Structure

Abstract

Proteins are complex molecules composed of one or more polypeptide chains made up of amino acid residues. These molecules perform a variety of essential functions in living organisms, including DNA replication, molecule transport, catalyzing metabolic processes, and providing structural support to cells. In this chapter, we explore the four levels of protein structure: primary, secondary, tertiary, and quaternary. Primary structure refers to the specific sequence of amino acids in a polypeptide chain, while secondary structure describes the folding of the chain into alpha-helices, beta-sheets, or other patterns. Tertiary structure is the three-dimensional shape of a single polypeptide chain, and quaternary structure refers to the interactions between multiple polypeptide chains to form a larger protein complex. Additionally, this chapter covers various methods used to predict protein structure, including homology modeling, ab initio prediction, and threading algorithms.

Introduction

Understanding protein structure is crucial due to the role of proteins as drug targets, enzymes, cell signaling, carrier molecules, etc. in various cellular activities. There are various levels of organization of protein structures, such as primary, secondary, etc.

Primary structure: a protein or polypeptide is a linear sequence of amino acids from the N-terminal to the C-terminal end.

Protein families: are evolutionarily related proteins that share common features or functions.

Secondary structure: is made up of regions that are held together by hydrogen bonds between atoms in the polypeptide backbone eg. α Helix and β Sheet.

Salient features of various secondary structures

α Helix

- It is the most abundant type of secondary structure in proteins.
- Architecture: Has 3.6 amino acids/ turn with an H bond formed between every fourth residue.
- Alignment of the H bonds creates a dipole moment for the helix with a resulting partial positive charge at the amino end of the helix.
- α-helices are prevalent at the surface of protein cores, since this portion provides an interface with the aqueous environment, due to the presence of free NH2 groups.
- The inner-facing side of the helix tends to have hydrophobic amino acids and the outer-facing side hydrophilic amino acids: thus every third of four amino acids along the chain tends to be hydrophobic.
- Regions richer in alanine (A), glutamic acid (E), leucine (L), and methionine (M) and poorer in proline (P), glycine (G), tyrosine (Y), and serine (S) tend to form α-helix.
- Proline destabilizes or breaks α-helix but can be present in longer helices, forming a bend.

β Sheet

- Architecture: formed by H bonding between 5–10 consecutive amino acids in one portion of the peptide chain with another 5–10 amino acids, located downward (nearby or somewhat distant) the chain
- Directions of the peptide chains:
    - Parallel sheet: every chain run in the same direction
    - Anti-parallel sheet: every other chain may run in the reverse chemical direction
    - Mixed sheet: chains may be a mixture of parallel and anti-parallel
- The H bonding pattern is different in the parallel and anti-parallel configurations.
- The Cα atoms alternate above and below the sheet in a pleated structure, and the R-side groups of the amino acids alternate above and below the pleats.

  - The Φ and Ψ angles of the amino acids in sheets vary considerably in one region of the Ramachandran plot
  - Prediction of β sheets is more challenging than that of α helices

- **Loop**
  - Features of loops:
    - Regions located between α helices and β sheets
    - Are of varying lengths and 3D configurations
    - Located on the surface of the structure: hence interact with the surrounding aqueous environment and other proteins
  - Hairpin loops: a complete turn in the polypeptide chain joining two antiparallel β strands
    - maybe as short as two amino acids in length
  - Loops may exhibit more substitutions, insertions, and deletions than the core region of the peptide chain due to
    - amino acids in loops are not constrained by space and environment as in the core region
    - do not affect the arrangement of secondary structures in the core
  - The amino acid in loops tend to have charged and polar amino acids

Coils: A region of secondary structure that is not α helix, a β sheet, or a recognizable turn is commonly referred to as a coil.

Tertiary structure: Tertiary structure is the three-dimensional shape of a protein determined by regions stabilized by side chain interactions. Protein tertiary structures are the result of weak interactions. Hydrophobic interactions among the amino acid side chains also determine the tertiary structure.

Hydrophilic Molecules: can dissolve in water and also know as water-loving molecules. They are polar.

Hydrophobic Molecules: can not dissolve in water and are also called water-repelling molecules. they are non-polar.

Quaternary structure: the association of two or more polypeptides. For example, hemoglobin has a molecular weight of 64,000 and is composed of four subunits, each with a molecular weight of 16,000. Salt bridges, hydrogen bonds, hydrophobic, and van der Waal's interaction act in an additive fashion to specifically associate subunits.

Denaturation and protein folding: Denatured protein lost their higher-order structure but not their primary sequence. Proteins that have been denatured are usually non-functional. Protein denaturation can be reversed to its functional form if it's returned to its normal environment.

Protein Structure prediction

Structural information from X-ray crystallographic or NMR results are obtained much more slowly and does not apply to all proteins. These techniques involve elaborate technical procedures, several proteins fail to crystallize at all and/or cannot be obtained or dissolved in large enough quantities for NMR measurements. The size of the protein is also a limiting factor for NMR. Therefore, protein structure prediction approaches were derived in the case of proteins with unknown structures. There are bioinformatics algorithms to predict the secondary, tertiary, and often quaternary structure of proteins from amino acid sequences. The applications of protein structure prediction can be found in therapeutics and personalized medicine, drug designing, and biotechnology (designing novel enzymes).

13

Homology Modeling

Abstract

When only sequence data is available, homology modeling has become a useful tool for predicting protein structure. Protein structure is often more important than sequence data when evaluating protein function. Homology modeling, also known as comparative modeling, is based on the principle that two sequences that exhibit a high degree of identity or similarity will also share similar structures. This chapter explores the steps involved in homology modeling, including template selection, alignment, model building, refinement, and validation. The Ramachandran plot is a valuable tool for assessing the conformation and bond angles in a protein model, and we discuss its significance in the context of homology modeling. Ultimately, homology modeling is an effective method for predicting protein structure and has numerous applications in protein engineering, drug discovery, and other fields.

Introduction

Homology modeling, also known as comparative modeling of a protein refers to constructing an atomic-resolution model of the "target" protein from its amino acid sequence and an experimental 3-D structure of a related homologous protein (the "template"). Knowledge of the homologous three-dimensional structure is essential for the structure prediction by homology modeling

Steps involved in homology modeling

Rotomers: Rotamers are the **low-energy side-chain conformations of peptide chains** forming a set of conformers arising from **restricted rotation around a single bond** during homology modeling. Protein backbone conformation has an intense impact on the rotamers (Chinea et al., 1995). These rotamers, a form of stereoisomer, are conformational isomers since the rotations about the single bonds produce the inter-convertible isomers. Determining the most accurate side-chain geometry is a challenging job. This can be addressed by using very high-resolution structures (~2.0 Å), filtering the false positive structures, etc. Rotamer-predicting platforms like YASARA utilizes the Phi(ϕ) and Psi(ψ) dihedral angles to extract the best-fitting rotamers and the probabilities obtained from a backbone-dependent rotamer library (Dunbrack RL Jr and Cohen, 1997).

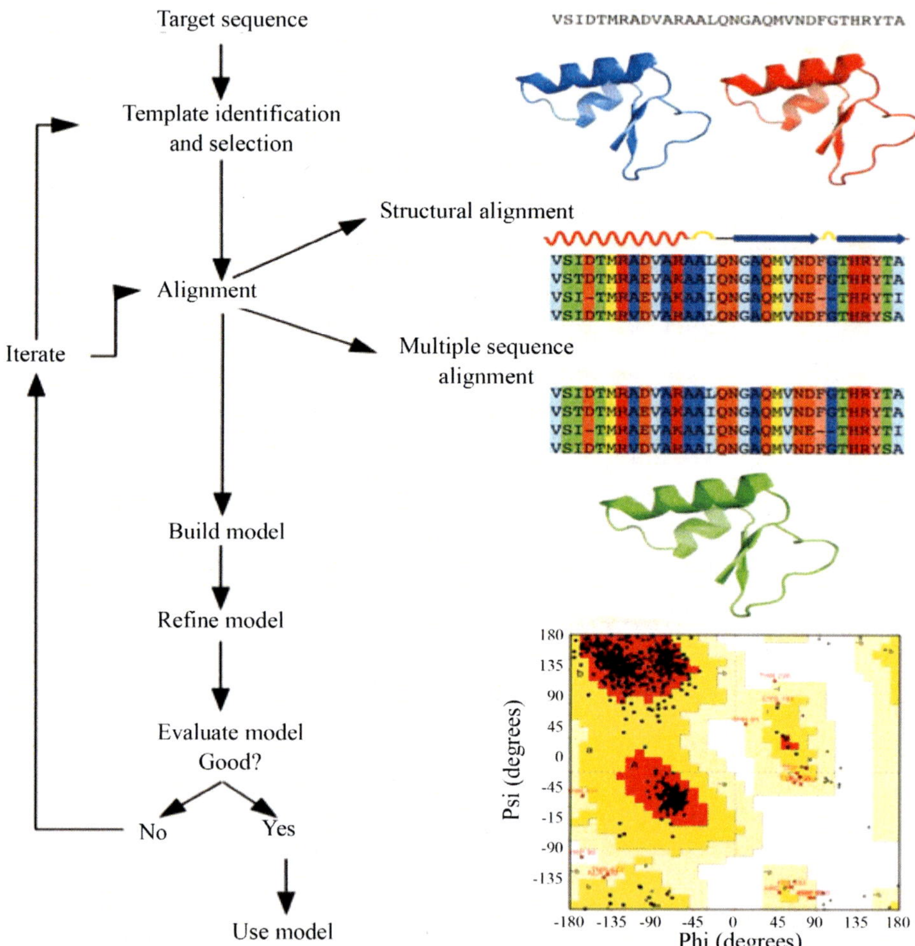

Ramachandran Plot and score

Ramachandran plots report the distribution of the (ϕ, ψ) torsion angles of the protein backbone and are one of the best quality metrics of experimental structure models. Validation of predicted and experimentally derived structures is performed using a Ramachandran plot, which reports the number of residues belonging to "outlier," "allowed," and "favored" regions, and the Ramachandran score is calculated, higher the score, the better the structure.

The Ramachandran plot is a diagrammatic visualization of protein structure by dihedral angles (psi (ψ) against phi (φ)) of amino acid residues. It was originally developed by a team of Ramachandran. It is a 2D graphical depiction of the plot between the peptide torsion angles Phi(ϕ) and Psi(ψ) in degrees. The dihedral angle of rotation about the alpha-carbon to carbonyl-carbon bond in polypeptides (i.e. Phi(ϕ)) is plotted against the dihedral angle of rotation about the alpha-carbon to nitrogen bond (i.e. Psi(ψ)) along the X and Y axes, respectively. It is used as a powerful tool to detect errors in predicted protein structure. The torsion angles are determined by considering the steric constraints from the van der Waals radii of each atom. Glycine residues are separately identified since these are not restricted to the regions of the plot like those of the other side-chain types.

This plot was first shown by G. R. Ramachandran in 1963 (G.N. Ramachandran, C. Ramakrishnan, and V. Sasisekharan. 1963. Stereochemistry of polypeptide chain configurations. *J Mol Biol.*, 7:95-9).

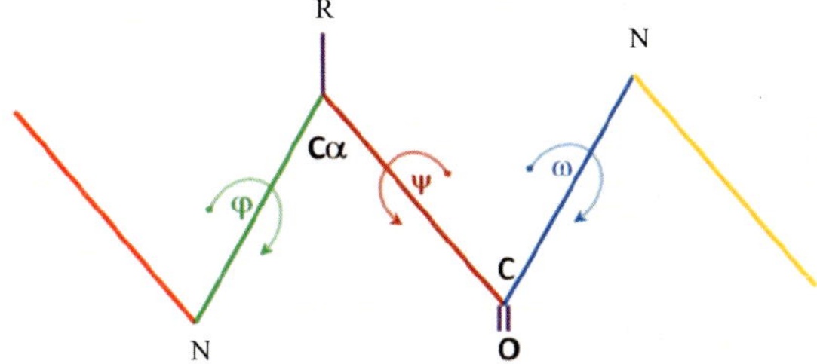

Peptide torsion angles evident in mainchain of a peptide: phi (j), psi (y) and omega (w)

Please note that the values of the phi and psi angles are negative and generally ranges between -60 to -50 degrees. The omega angle is morstly restricted to 180 degrees due to the planarity of the peptide bond. In contrast, in case of proline the omega angle is zero degrees (for the cis peptide bond).

14

Molecular Modeling

Abstract

Molecular modeling is a computational technique used to simulate the three-dimensional interactions between atoms and molecules. It allows for the visualization, manipulation, and prediction of molecular structures and chemical reactions. In this chapter, we discuss the different types of molecular models used in computational chemistry, including ball-and-stick models, space-filling models, wireframe models, and ribbon models. Ball-and-stick models depict atoms as spheres and bonds as sticks. Molecular modeling has numerous applications in drug discovery, materials science, and other fields of research, making it a valuable tool for computational chemists and molecular biologists. Here, this chapter focuses on different types of molecular models.

Molecular Modeling (MM)

MM is a collection of computer-based techniques for driving, representing, and manipulating molecule structures and reactions, as well as the properties that depend on these 3D structures. It helps in determining the physicochemical properties that can help to interpret the structural activity relationship (SAR) of the biological molecules.

In the 1600s, Johannes Kepler hypothesized about the symmetry of snowflakes as well as the close packing of spherical objects like fruit (this problem remained unsolved until very recently). In the late 1800s, the symmetrical arrangement of closely packed spheres informed theories of molecular structure, and many crystallographic and solid-state inorganic structure theories used collections of equal and unequal spheres to simulate packing and predict structure.

Molecular modeling provides five major types of information.

- The 3D structure of molecules.
- The chemical and physical characteristics of the molecules.
- Comparison of the structure of a molecule with other different molecules.

- Visualization of complexes formed between different. molecules/ macromolecules.
- Prediction about how new related molecules might look.

Types of Molecular Models

- **Ball and spike models:** Ball and spoke models are a common way of representing molecular structures. Each atom is represented by a colored ball that is joined to other atoms using spokes to represent the bonds between them. This type of model emphasizes the bonding between atoms.
- **Space-filling models**: Space-filling models depict the overall size and shape of the molecule, indicating (relatively) how much space each atom occupies. H. A. Stuart invented the space-filling model in 1934.
- **Crystal lattice models:** Molecular model kits are intended to be reused; models can be built and then disassembled, but chemists frequently construct permanent models of molecular structures for demonstrations or teaching. Mr. C. E. Chapman, the Chief technician of the Crystallography Department, part of the Cavendish Laboratory at the University of Cambridge, created this crystallographic model of the metal beta-manganese around 1952. It depicts how manganese atoms are arranged at high temperatures.

The techniques address a variety of issues, including computational chemistry, drug design, computational biology, nanostructures, and material science.

- **Molecular mechanics:** The force fields are the methods of choice for protein simulations, this is essential in the study of conformational flexibility. Molecular mechanics can be applied to the study of molecule systems ranging in size and complexity from small to large biological systems or material assemblies containing thousands to millions of atoms.

Force field: A force field is a mathematical expression that describes the dependence of a system's energy on the coordinates of its particles. It is made up of an analytical form of the interatomic potential energy, U(r1, r2,..., rN), as well as a set of parameters that enter into this form.

15

Drug Designing

Abstract

Drug design is a complex computational process that involves studying the structural and physicochemical properties of biological moieties in order to identify new chemical or biochemical substances that can be used as drugs with specific pharmacological properties. The drug discovery pipeline is a crucial aspect of drug design that requires a detailed understanding of the various phases involved. In this chapter, we discuss the fundamental principles and phases of drug design. Additionally, we delve into the concept of docking, a critical step in the drug discovery process that involves predicting the orientation and affinity of a ligand binding to a protein target. The use of computational tools and techniques in drug design has revolutionized the field and is essential for the development of safe and effective drugs.

Drug Designing: Drug can be defined as any organic or inorganic molecule with the ability to activate or inhibit biological function of any biomolecule in the body to induce therapeutic benefit to the patient. Drug designing is a lengthy process that invlolves both biocomputational and laboratory experimental steps for identifying molecules that are complementary in shape and charge to the biomolecular target with which they interact and therefore will bind to it.

Types of Drug Designing

- Ligand-based drug designing: It is also called as indirect drug designing that relies on properties of other molecules that can interact and bind to the biological target(s). Thereby, ligand based drug designing can identify new molecular entities that interact with the target.
- Structure-based drug designing: is the most powerful drug-lead discovery process. It is an iterative process. It is based on understanding the three-dimensional structure of the drug and how its shape and charge cause it to interact with its biological target, ultimately eliciting a medical effect.
- Rational drug discovery (RDD): begins with a hypothesis that modulation of a specific biological target may have therapeutic value.

- Computer-assisted drug design (CADD): can be combined with wet-lab techniques to elucidate the mechanism of drug resistance, to search for new antibiotic targets and to design novel antibiotics for both known and new targets. CADD methods can produce an atomic level structure-activity relationship (SAR) used to facilitate the drug design process thereby minimizing time and costs.

Why *in-silico* Drug Design is significant?

- Structure determination by computational tools.
- Identify and analyze active sites.
- Reduce time and cost.
- Design superior drugs.

Drug Discovery Pipeline

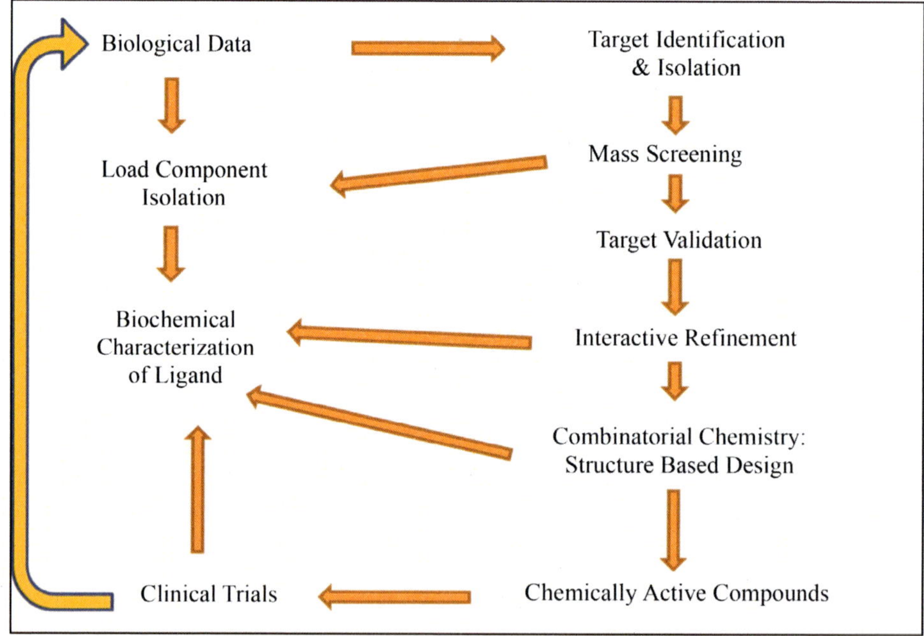

Drug Discovery and Development Process

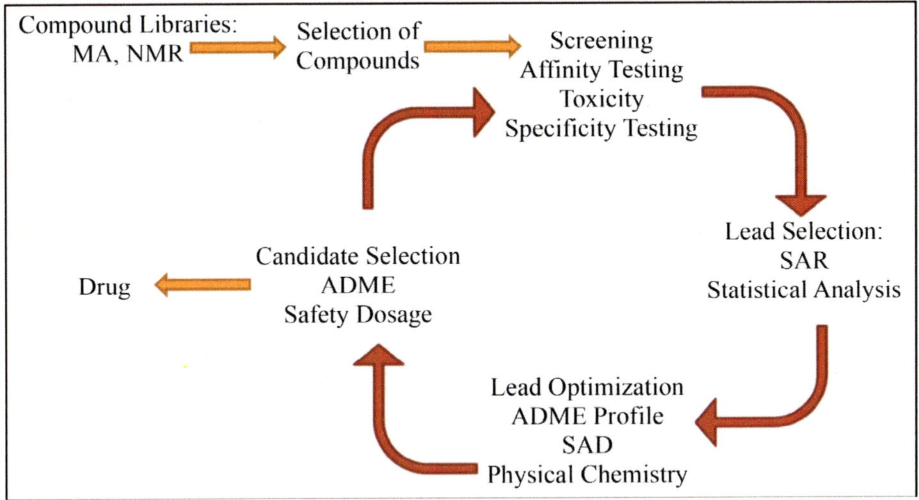

Please be acquainted with some of the important terms in bioinformatics as below

Docking: is to identify and understand the methods by which the active site of a receptor selectively checks the binding of the inappropriate structures. A receptor is a protein molecule, capable of selectively binding a ligand, viz. drug, hormone, or neurotransmitter, to elicit a physiological response. Any molecule that can bind to a receptor is called a ligand, in a **key (ligand)** in the **lock (receptor)** orientation. Thus, the molecular key comprises an explicit combination of atoms that enables it to bind and interact with the receptor due to steric complementarity between the ligand and the receptor binding sites. Steric complementarity can be explained as the complementarity of size and shape between the ligand and receptor in such a manner that the shape of the ligand is imaged in the shape of the binding site vis-à-vis the physio-chemical complementarity that allows molecular interactions between them since ligand should contain complementary charged atoms in the appropriate orientation for their proper binding (http://www.newdrugdesign.com/Rachel_Theory_02.html).

In bioinformatics, docking is a computational simulation of a ligand binding to its receptor.

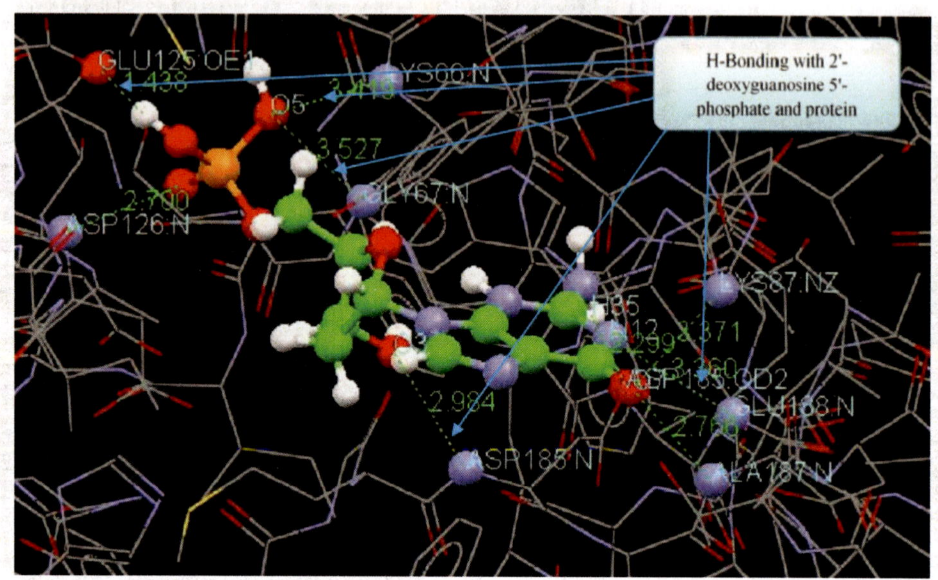

Protein ligands docking in GOLD

Molecular dynamics and Simulation: First, the best model is selected out of all predicted structures then, the structure is stabilized in a water medium as the cellular medium is aqueous using MD simulation. MD is a way of solving equations of motion numerically, Molecular dynamics (MD) is a computer simulation method for analyzing the physical movements of atoms and molecules.

"Absorption, Distribution, Metabolism, and Excretion" (ADME) aims at investigating the processing and metabolism of a drug compound by a living organism.

Quantitative structure-activity relationship (QSAR) models are kind of regression or classification models used in the chemical and biological sciences to predict the biological effects of chemical compounds.

History and evolution of molecular dynamics (MD)

- 1953: Metropolis Monte Carlo (MC) by Metropolis, Rosenbluth, Rosenbluth, Teller, and Teller –simulation of a dense liquid of 2D spheres
- 1955: Fermi, Pasta, and Ulam –simulation of an anharmonic 1D crystal
- 1956: Alder and Wainwright –molecular dynamics (MD) simulation of hard spheres (1958: First X-ray structure of a protein)

- 1960: Vineyard group – Simulation of damaged Cu crystal.
- 1964: Rahman –MD simulation of liquid Ar
- 1969: Barker and Watts –Monte Carlo simulation of water
- 1971: Rahman and Stillinger –MD simulation of water
- 1972: I.R. McDonald - NPT simulation using Monte Carlo

16

Systems Biology

Abstract

Systems biology is an interdisciplinary field that combines computer and mathematical analysis with biological research to understand the complex interactions within biological systems. This chapter explores the history and evolution of systems biology and its significant impact on modern biology. Systems biology uses a holistic approach to analyze biological systems at the molecular, cellular, and organismal levels, providing a better understanding of biological processes and the interactions between genes, proteins, and other molecules. Systems biology has immense potential in improving human health, agriculture, and the environment, and this chapter explores the ongoing efforts to translate systems biology research into practical applications.

The computer and mathematical analysis and modelling of complex biological systems is known as systems biology. It is a biology-based interdisciplinary field of study that focuses on complex interactions within biological systems and takes a comprehensive approach to biological research. This chapter covers the history and revolution in systems biology, significance of system biology and its application in biology.

Systems Biology: "*Every object that biology study is a system of systems.*" Francois Jacob (1974).

- Systems biology is a quantitative investigation of how all of the components of a biological system interact functionally over time. It is also known as "Integrative Biology", which comprises computational and mathematical analysis and modeling of complex biological systems with the fundamental objective to predict de novo biological outcomes given the list of components involved.
- The study of systems has had a huge impact on what is loosely referred to as human sciences, such as economics, sociology, psychology, and medicine.

- Systems biology has revolutionized ecology, population biology, and evolutionary studies, and it is slowly infiltrating biochemistry, development, genetics, and whole-plant biology.

History of Systems Biology

- 1968: The term systems biology was introduced by Mihajlo Mesarovic (Mesarovic, 1968, Mesarovic et al., 2004).
- 2000: It has begun as a new field of science when the Institute for Systems Biology was established in Seattle to lure "computational" people.
- 2001: The international project "Physiome" has become an important milestone in the development of systems biology.
- 2003: A Department of Systems Biology at Harvard Medical School was launched.
- 2006: the National Science Foundation put forward a challenge to build a mathematical model of the whole cell.
- 2012: the first whole-cell model of *Mycoplasma genitalium* was achieved by the Karr Laboratory at the Mount Sinai School of Medicine in New York.

Why study Systems Biology

- A living cell can be viewed as a dynamical system in which a large number of different substances interact with one another in a continuous and nonlinear fashion.
- Because it is insufficient to study each component separately, With the help of the system biology approach, it is possible to observe time-domain concentrations of substances and automatically generate the topology of the network of chemical reactions as well as the rates of each reaction.
- Define each gene's, RNA's, and protein's interactions.
- Decipher each reaction in this metabolic network.
- To investigate the action and behavior of each molecule comprising dynamic, boolean, digraph, and network models.

Applications

- Systems Biology is an emerging field that has the potential to make a significant contribution to human life in applications in different domains such as drug targeting, drug designing, interpreting basic principles, and prediction of disease conditions, etc.

- Examining large-scale gene expression data from a variety of diseases to find gene markers and disease sub-categories.
- To develop theoretical models of gene regulatory networks and reconstruct and integrate active protein interaction and metabolic networks.

Gene ontology: is the functional annotation, assimilation, and dissemination of information of gene and gene products across all species.

17

Synthetic Biology

Abstract

Synthetic biology is a multidisciplinary field of study that seeks to understand living systems and organisms, and utilizes engineering principles to design and create new biological components, devices, and systems, as well as modify existing natural systems. This chapter provides an introduction to synthetic biology and describes the procedures and methodologies involved in the design and construction of novel biological systems. The applications of synthetic biology are vast and include the development of biosensors, gene circuits, metabolic pathways, and genetically modified organisms for use in a variety of industries, including healthcare, agriculture, energy, and environmental remediation.

Synthetic biology: An emerging interdisciplinary field in which engineering principles are applied to biology. Its goal is to redesign and fabricate biological components and systems that do not currently exist in nature. The term "synthetic biology" was first coined in 1980. Synthetic biology experimented with the idea of creating "made-to-order" microbes from well-studied biological components.

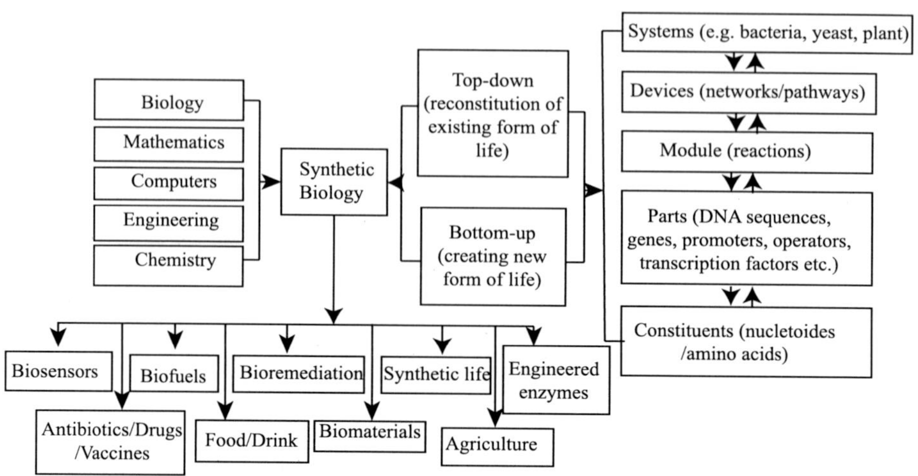

An overview of synthetic biology showing the combination of fields, with which it associates, and its wide applicability (https://doi.org/10.1016/B978-0-444-64085-7.00001-0).

Applications: Identity and catalog standardized genomic parts that can be used (and synthesized quickly) to build novel biological systems. Re-design existing biological parts and expand the set of natural protein functions for new processes with applied protein design.

Natural product synthesis: Engineer microbes to produce all of the necessary enzymes and biological functions to perform complex multistep.

Synthetic genomics: Design and build a much simple genome for a natural bacterium.